YES, this is a "BLURB"!

All the Other Publishers commit them.   Why Shouldn't We?

MISS
BELINDA
BLURB

IN
THE ACT OF
BLURBING

ARE YOU A BROMIDE?

BY

GELETT BURGESS

Say! Ain't this book a 90-H. P., six-cylinder Seller? If WE do say it as shouldn't, WE consider that this man Burgess has got Henry James locked into the coal-bin, telephoning for " Information "

WE expect to sell 350 copies of this great, grand book. It has gush and go to it, it has that Certain Something which makes you want to crawl through thirty miles of dense tropical jungle and bite somebody in the neck.   No hero no heroine, nothing like that for OURS, but when you've *READ* this masterpiece, you'll know what a BOOK is, and you'll sic it onto your mother-in-law, your dentist and the pale youth who dips hot-air into Little Marjorie until 4 Q. M. in the front parlour.   This book has 42-carat THRILLS in it.   It fairly BURBLES. Ask the man at the counter what HE thinks of it! He's seen Janice Meredith faded to a mauve magenta.   He's seen BLURBS before, and he's dead wise.   He'll say:

This Book is the Proud Purple Penultimate ! !

Overleaf:

In addition to writing numerous books about the Goops, Gelett Burgess took great pride in writing nonsense. He actually coined the term "blurb" in this advertisement for his book *Are you a Bromide?* in which he defines a Bromide as follows:

> "The Bromide does his thinking by syndicate. He follows the main traveled roads, he goes with the crowd. In a word, they all think and talk alike--one may predicate their opinion upon any given subject. They follow custom and costume, they obey the Law of Averages. They are, intellectually, all peas in the same conventional pod, unenlightened, prosaic, living by rule and rote. They have their hair cut every month and their minds keep regular office hours. Their habits of thought are all ready-made, proper, sober, befitting the Average Man. They worship dogma. The Bromide conforms to everything sanctioned by the majority, and may be depended upon to be trite, banal and arbitrary."

In a book that seeks to introduce Gelett Burgess' "race void of beauty and of grace" to a new generation, what more appropriate way than to let him supply his own "blurb"?

I NEVER SAW A PURPLE COW I NEVER HOPE TO SEE ONE

BUT I CAN TELL YOU ANYHOW ID RATHER SEE THAN BE ONE

More about Gelett Burgess:

Born in Boston in 1866, Burgess graduated with a B.S. from MIT and began his career as a draftsman for the Southern Pacific Railroad, followed by a position as a drafting instructor at the University of California at Berkley in 1891. By 1895, his talent for writing and drawing had led him to start a magazine called *The Lark*. The very first issue featured the nonsense poem "the Purple Cow," (shown above) which would eventually become his trademark.

In 1900, he published *Goops and How to Be Them*, giving life to a set of characters that he would continue to develop over several decades, through numerous books and even a comic strip. His uniquely humorous take on the serious subject of manners has delighted generations and even served as an inspiration for later authors, most notably the king of nonsense, Dr. Seuss.

A COLLECTION
OF
GOOPS

"You can repeat nonsense all your life and never get tired of it, but you can't do the same thing with Browning."

--Gelett Burgess

A COLLECTION OF GOOPS

CONTAINING:

GOOPS
AND HOW TO BE THEM

~

MORE GOOPS
AND HOW NOT TO BE
THEM

~

AN ALPHABET OF
FAMOUS GOOPS

BY GELETT BURGESS

ST. AUGUSTINE ACADEMY PRESS
LISLE, ILLINOIS

This volume is a compilation of two previously published books and an excerpt from a third.
Goops and How to Be Them was originally published in 1900.
More Goops and How Not to Be Them was originally published in 1903.
"An Alphabet of Famous Goops" is taken from *The Burgess Nonsense Book*, published in 1901.
All were published by Frederick A Stokes Company.

This edition ©2012 by St. Augustine Academy Press.

ISBN: 978-1-936639-14-4
Library of Congress Control Number: 2012932279

All illustrations in this volume, including the cover,
are the original illustrations as found in the books listed above.
The frontispiece and overleaf illustrations were taken from contemporary sources now in the public domain.

CONTENTS

GOOPS
AND HOW TO BE THEM

A Manual of Manners for Polite Infants
Inculcating many Juvenile Virtues
Both by Precept and Example
With Ninety Drawings

By GELETT BURGESS

To Agnes
who is
Not
(always)
a Goop!

TABLE OF CONTENTS

TABLE OF CONTENTS

Of these Rhymes, ten first appeared in
"St. Nicholas," *and are here reprinted*
by permission of the Century Company

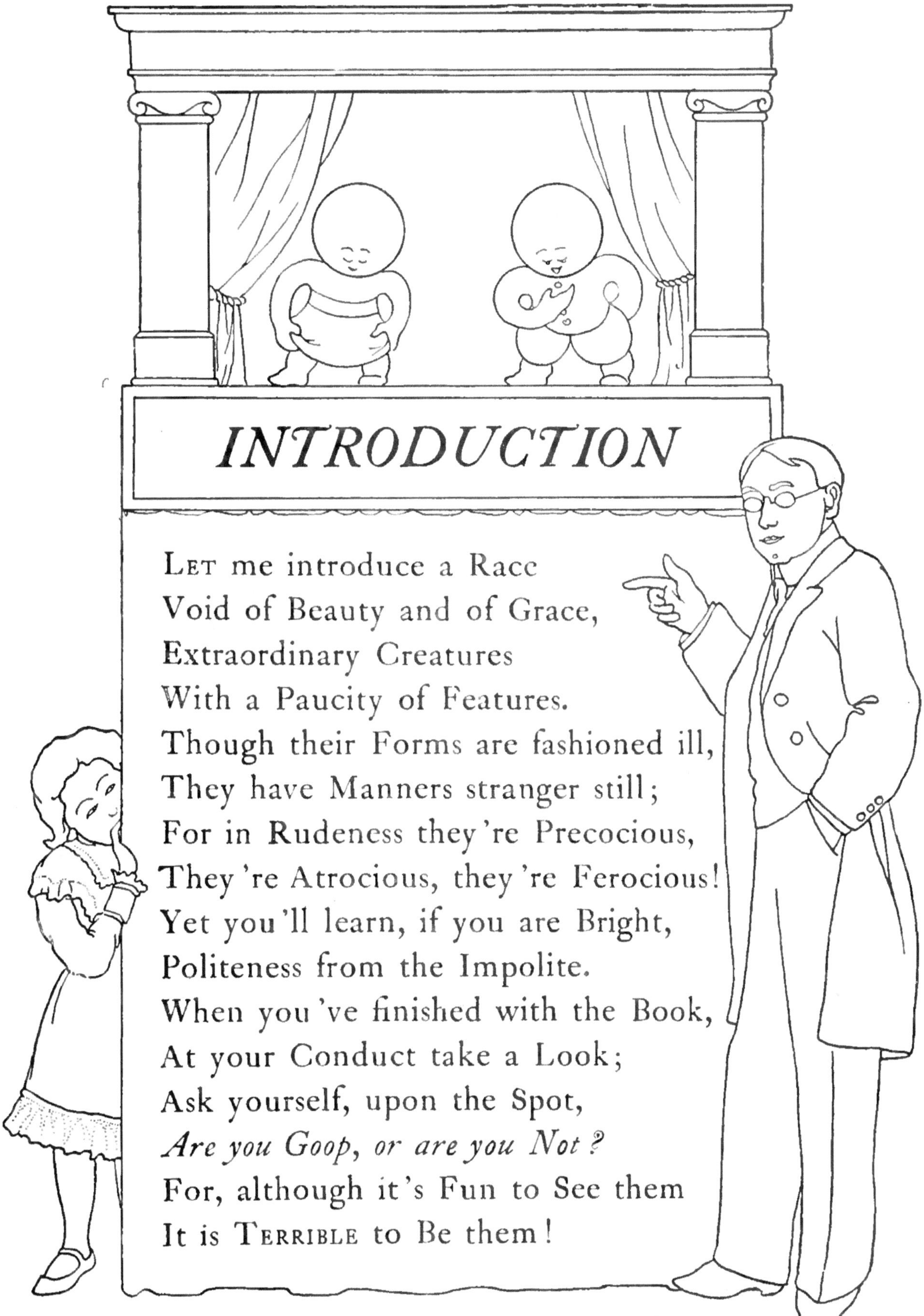

INTRODUCTION

Let me introduce a Race
Void of Beauty and of Grace,
Extraordinary Creatures
With a Paucity of Features.
Though their Forms are fashioned ill,
They have Manners stranger still;
For in Rudeness they're Precocious,
They're Atrocious, they're Ferocious!
Yet you'll learn, if you are Bright,
Politeness from the Impolite.
When you've finished with the Book,
At your Conduct take a Look;
Ask yourself, upon the Spot,
Are you Goop, or are you Not?
For, although it's Fun to See them
It is Terrible to Be them!

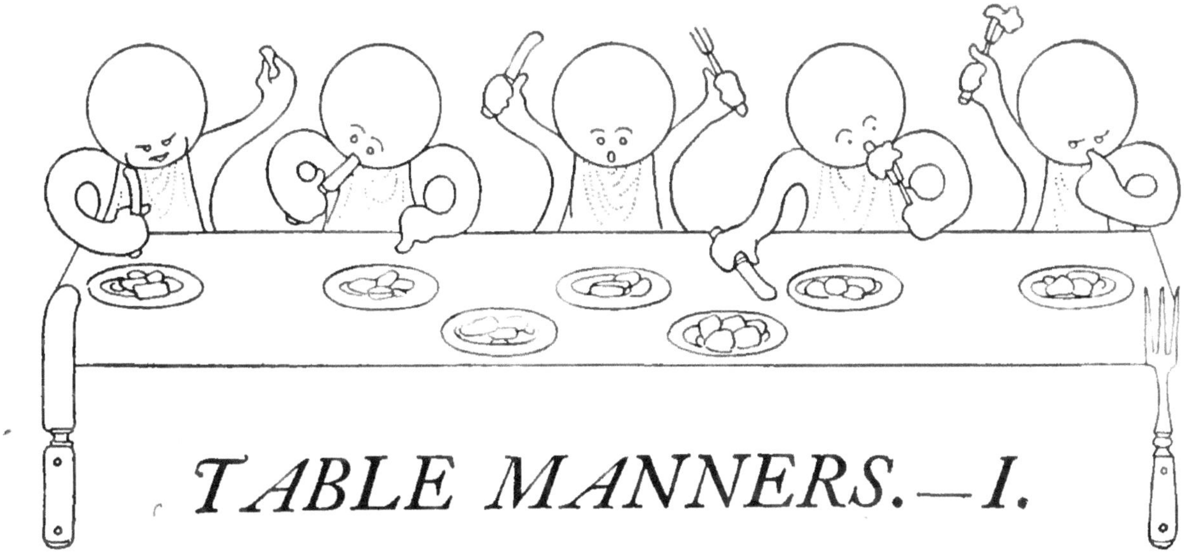

TABLE MANNERS.—I.

THE Goops they lick their fingers,
And the Goops they lick their
knives;
They spill their broth on the table-
cloth—
Oh, they lead disgusting lives!
The Goops they talk while eating,
And loud and fast they chew;
And that is why I 'm glad that I
Am not a Goop—are you?

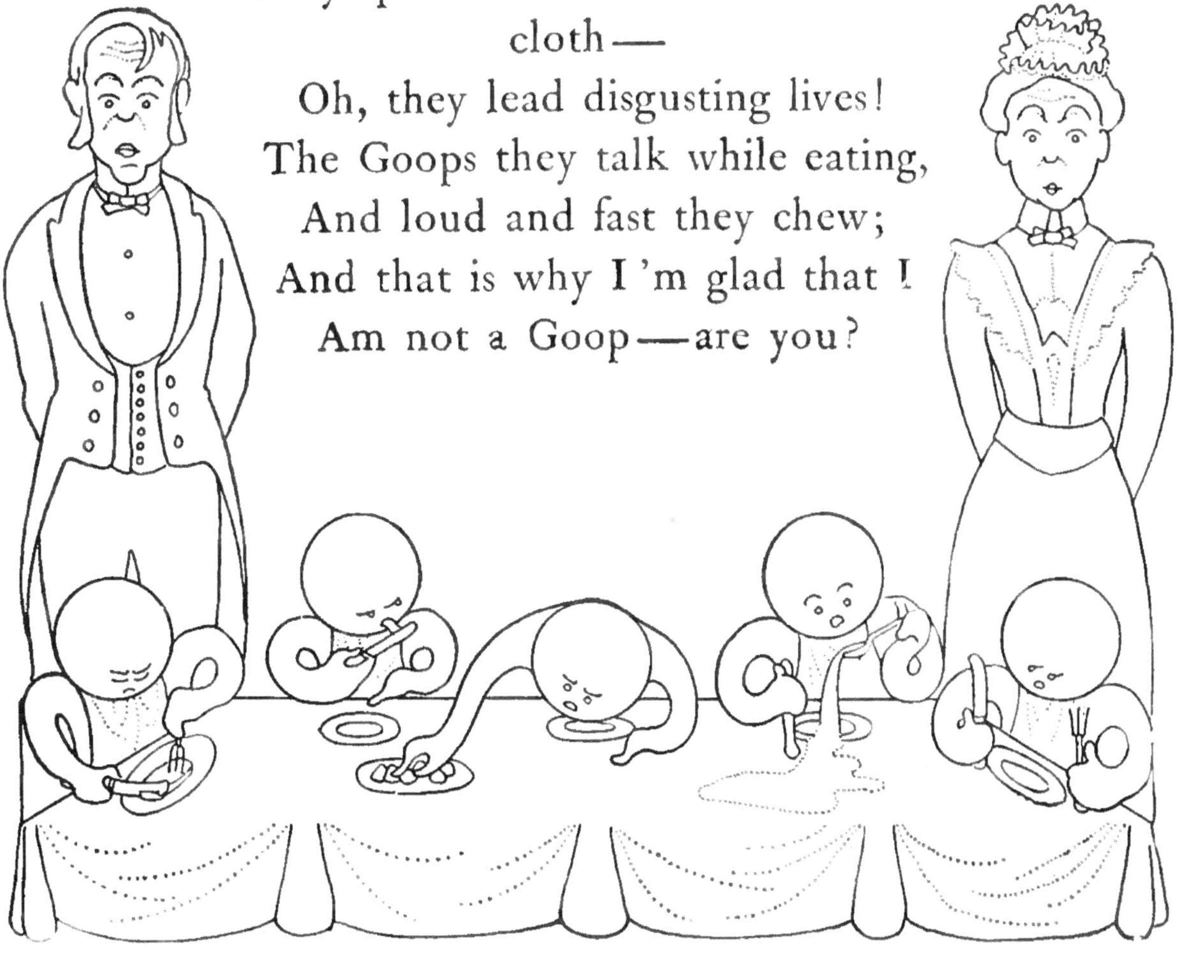

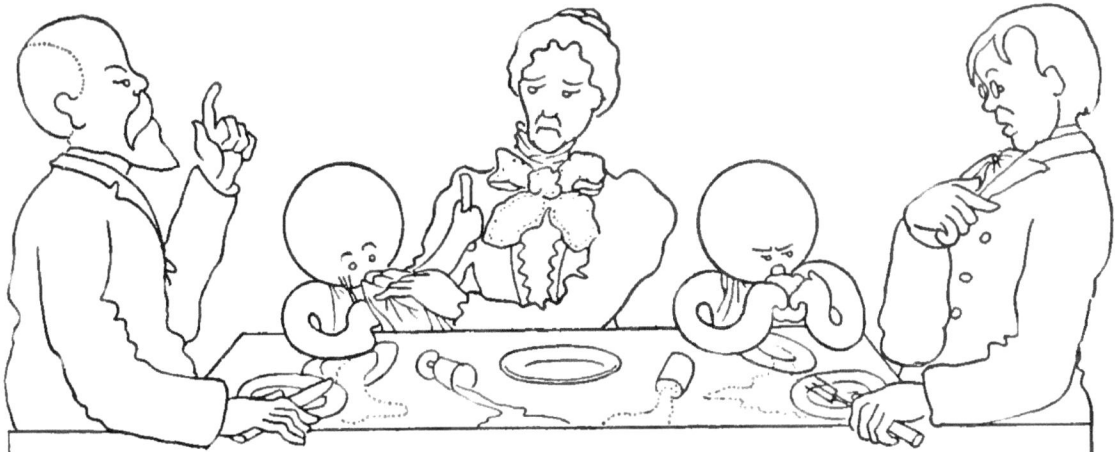

TABLE MANNERS.—II.

THE Goops are gluttonous and rude,
They gug and gumble with their food;
They throw their crumbs upon the floor,
And at dessert they tease for more;
They will not eat their soup and bread
But like to gobble sweets, instead,
And this is why I oft decline,
When I am asked to stay and dine!

CLEANLINESS

THE Goops they are spotted on chin and on cheek,
  You could dig the dirt off with a trowel!
But *you* wash your face twenty times every week,
  And you don't do it *all* with the towel!

The Goops are all dirty, and what do they do?
  They like to be dirty, and stay so.
But if *you* were dirty, you'd wash, wouldn't you?
  If you needed a bath, you would say so!

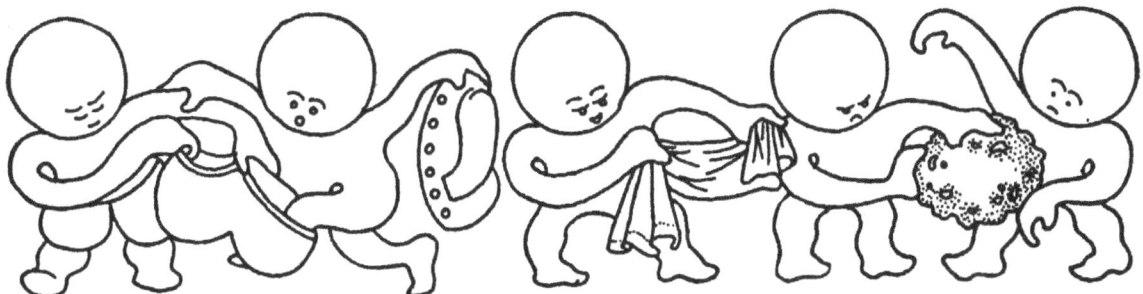

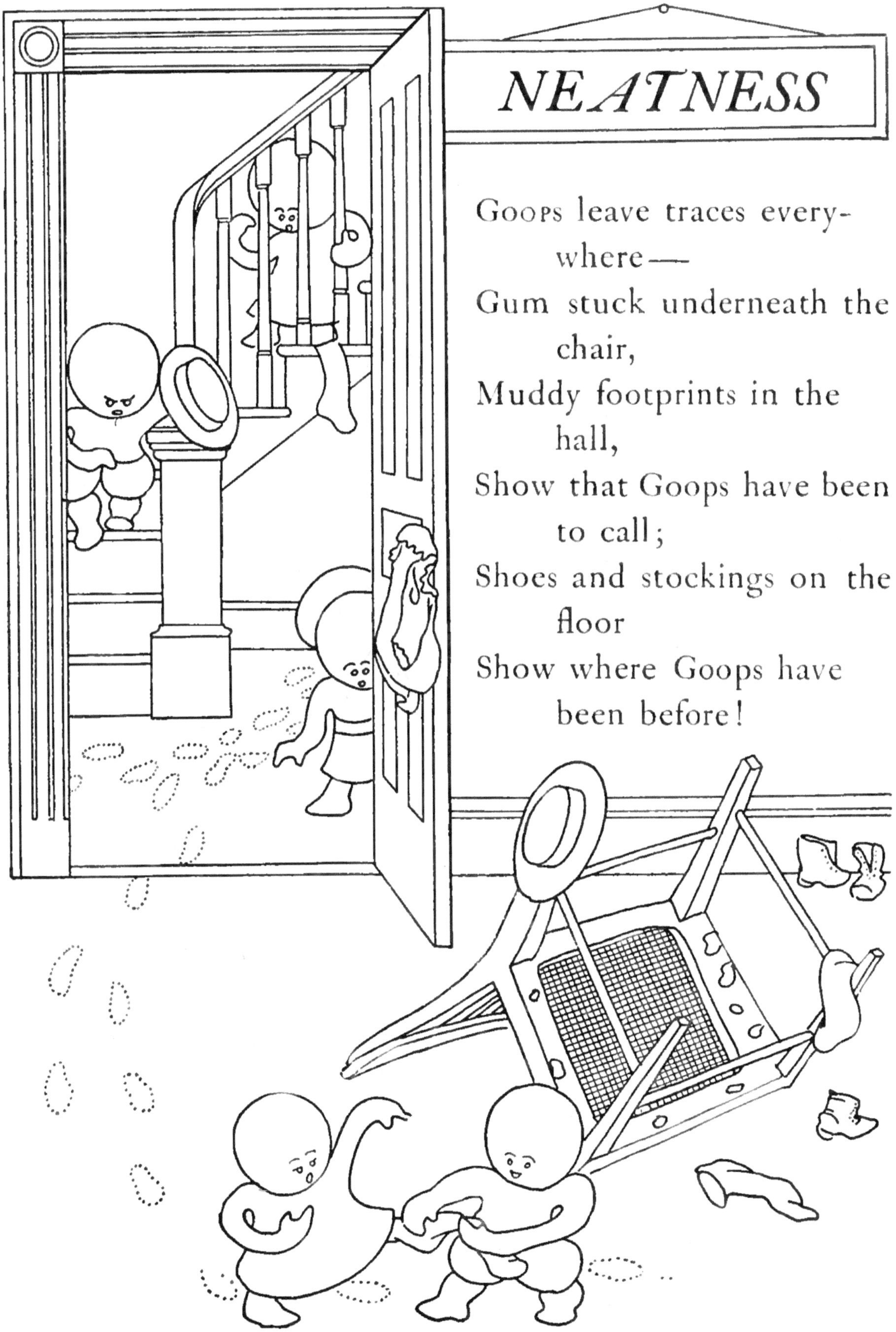

NEATNESS

Goops leave traces every-
where—
Gum stuck underneath the
chair,
Muddy footprints in the
hall,
Show that Goops have been
to call;
Shoes and stockings on the
floor
Show where Goops have
been before!

COURTESY

I WONDER why it is polite
In shaking hands, to give your *right*.
I wonder why it is refined
In passing one, to go *behind*.
I wonder why it is well-bred,
If you must sneeze, to turn your head.
Perhaps the reason is because
The Goops, they never have such laws!

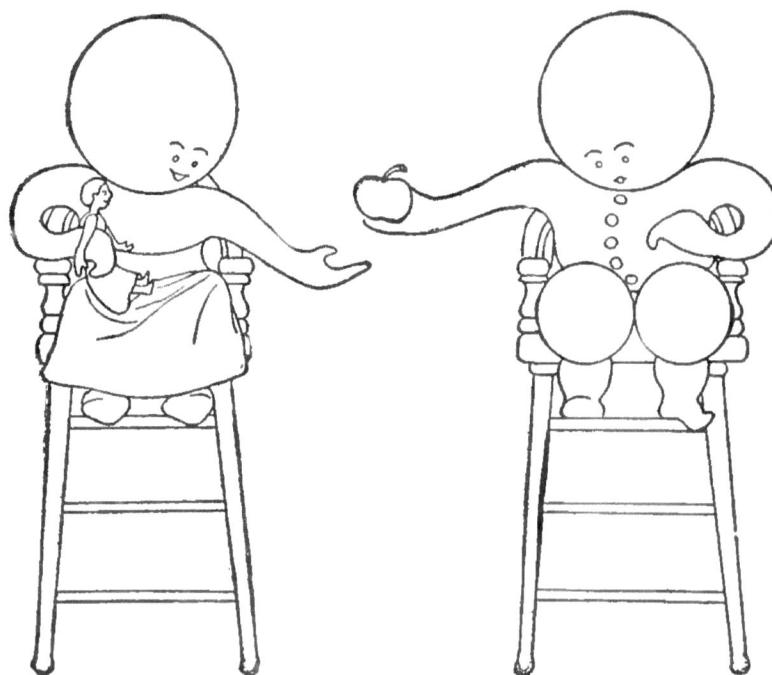

GENEROSITY

WHEN you have candy, do you go
And give your sister half?
When little brother stubs his toe,
Do you look on and laugh?

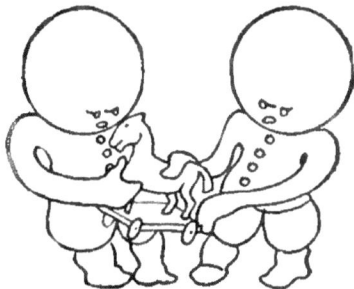

The greediest Goop would give away
The things he didn't need —
To share the toys with which you play,
That's generous, indeed!

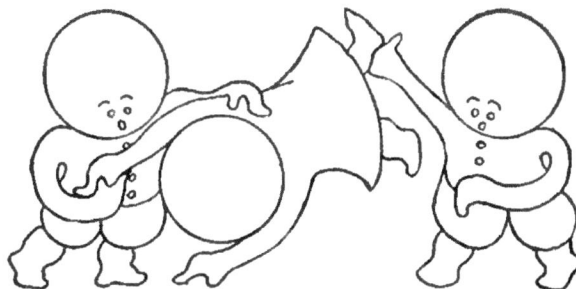

CONSIDERATION

WHEN you 're old, and get to be
Thirty-four or forty-three,
Don't you hope that you will see
Children all respect you?

Will they, without being told,
Wait on you, when you are old,
Or be heedless, selfish, cold?
I *hope* they 'll not neglect
you!

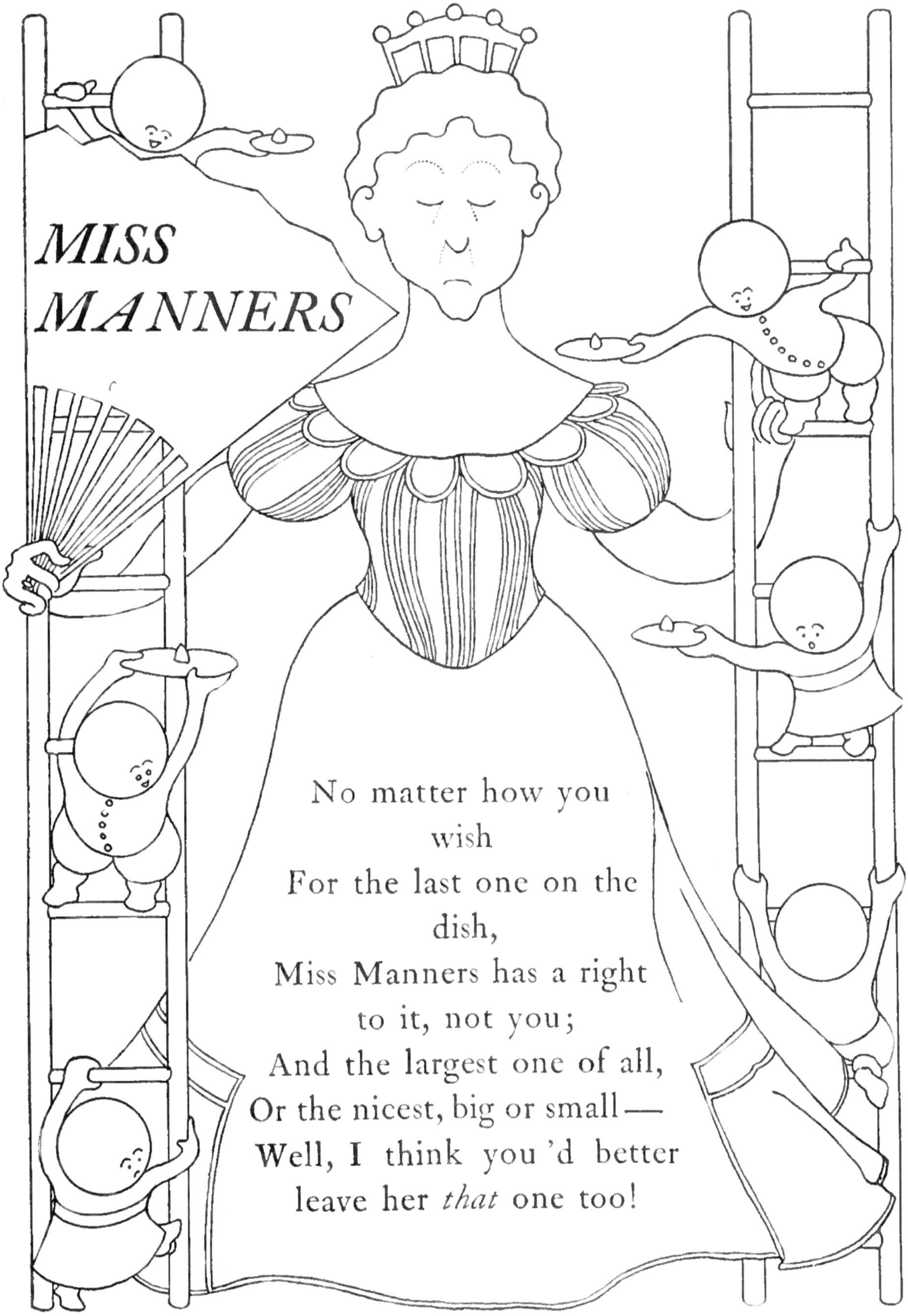

MISS MANNERS

No matter how you
wish
For the last one on the
dish,
Miss Manners has a right
to it, not you;
And the largest one of all,
Or the nicest, big or small—
Well, I think you 'd better
leave her *that* one too!

BORROWING

WHOSE doll is that on the table?
    Whose book is that on the chair?
The knife and the pencils and other
      utensils,
    Now how do they come to be there?

Did n't you say they were borrowed?
    You'd better take back just a few!
If *you* lent your playthings, I think
      you would say things
    If no one returned them to you!

A B C D E F G H I
J K L M N O P Q R
S T U V W X Y Z &
1 2 3 4 5 6 7 8 9

MEMORY

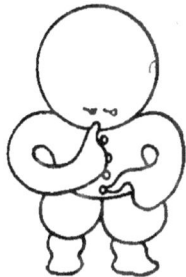

My teacher taught me, yesterday,
A very pretty piece to say;
But when I try to think of it,
I can't remember it a bit!
My head's so full of toys and such,
I can't remember very much!

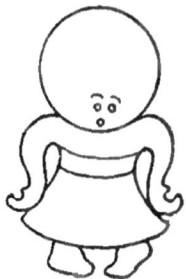

My teacher told me yesterday
"*Work when you work;*
Play when you play!"
When I am playing with my toys
I am the busiest of boys;
But when I study or I work
I'm 'fraid I *am* inclined to shirk!

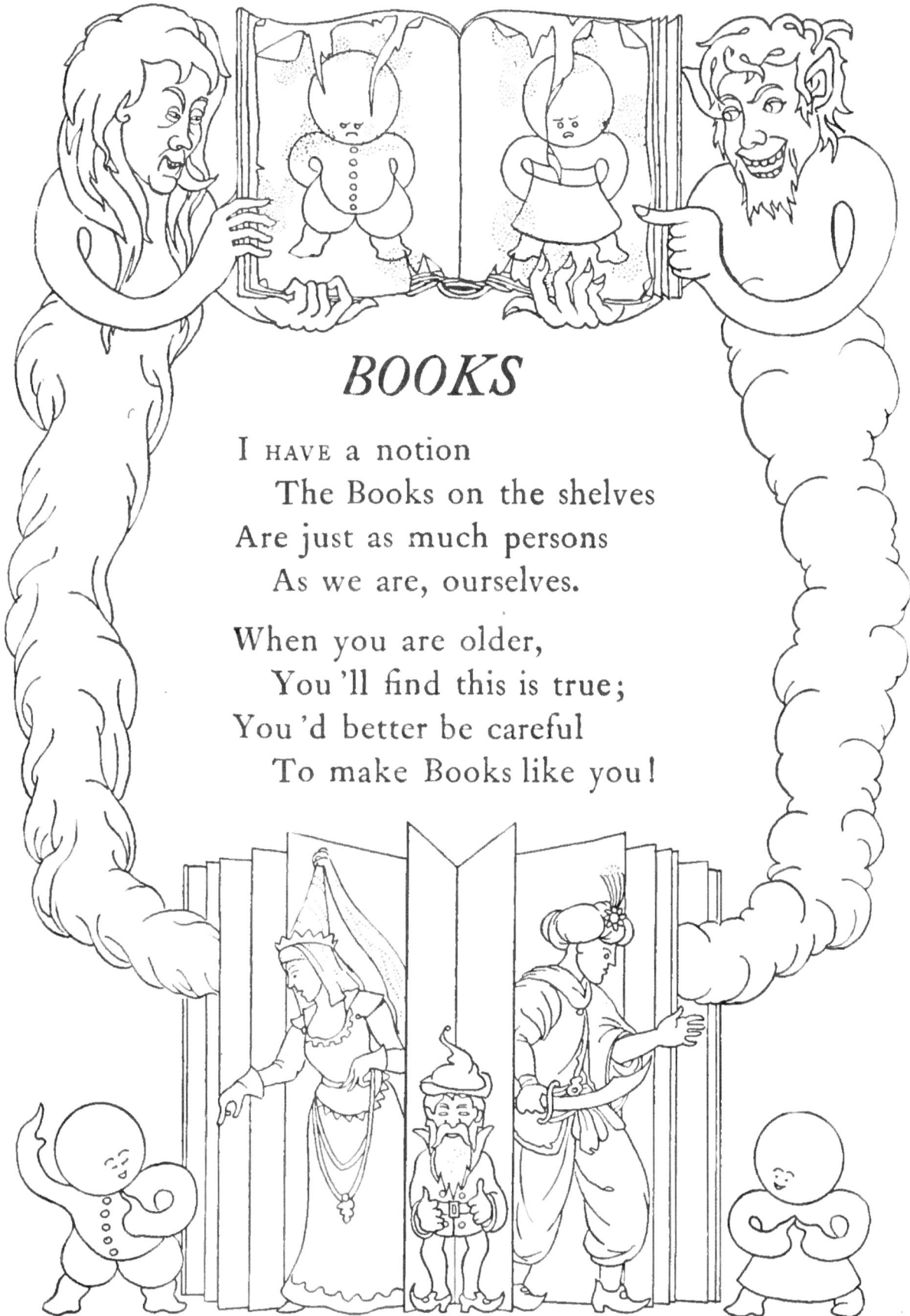

BOOKS

I HAVE a notion
    The Books on the shelves
Are just as much persons
    As we are, ourselves.

When you are older,
    You'll find this is true;
You'd better be careful
    To make Books like you!

HONESTY

THE boy who plays at marbles and does n't try to cheat,
Who always keeps his temper, no matter if he's beat,
Is sure to be a favorite with all upon the street.

The girl who counts her hundreds very fairly, when she's "it"
Who does n't peep or listen, nor turn around a bit,
I'm sure she's not a Goop, in fact, she's quite the opposite!

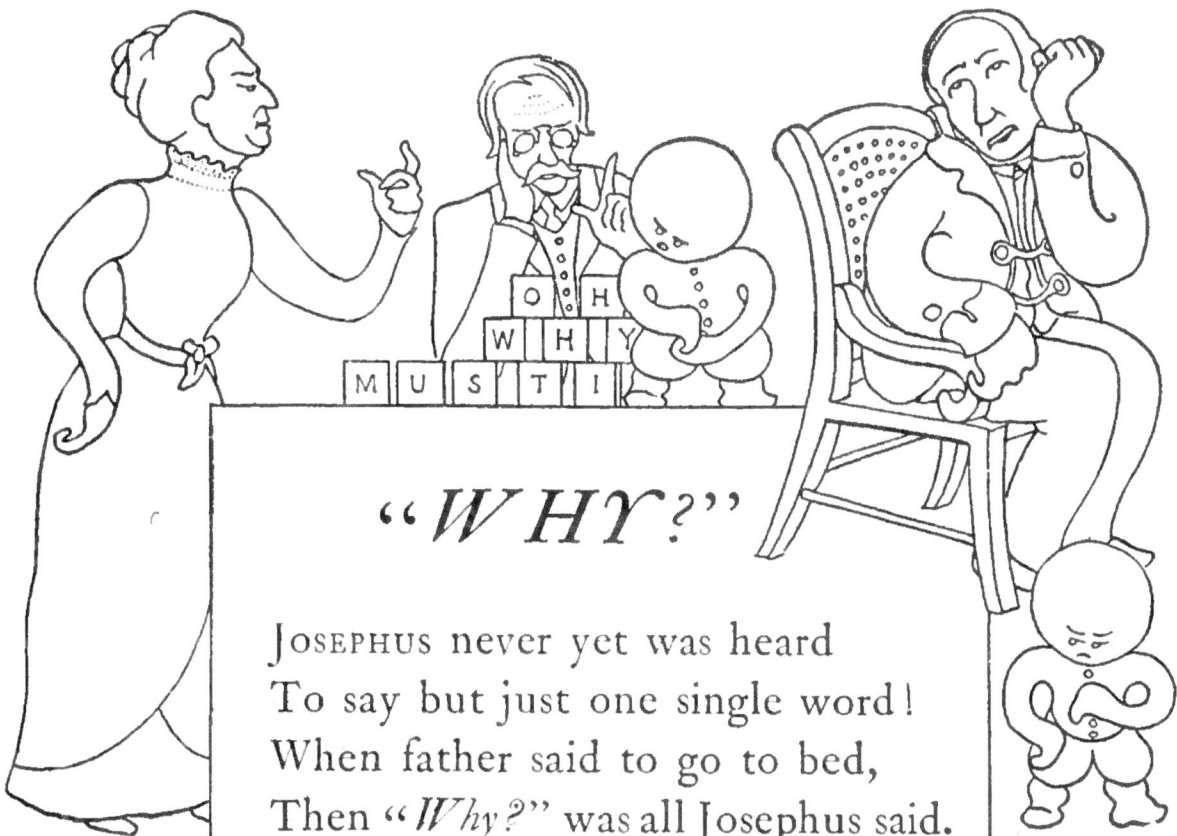

"WHY?"

JOSEPHUS never yet was heard
To say but just one single word!
When father said to go to bed,
Then "*Why?*" was all Josephus said.
When mother bade him stop his play,
Then "*Why?*" Josephus used to say.
He always made the same reply.
'T was never anything but
"WHY?"

BED-TIME

THE night is different from the day—
It's darker in the night;
How can you ever hope to play
When it's no longer light?

When bed-time comes, it's time for you
To stop, for when you're yawning,
You should be dreaming what you'll do
When it's to-morrow morning.

MODESTY

THE proper time for you to show
Whatever little tricks you know
Is when grown people ask you to;
Then you may show what you
                can do!
But sometimes mother's head
                will ache
With all the jolly noise you make,
And sometimes other people, too,
Can't spend the time to play
                with you!

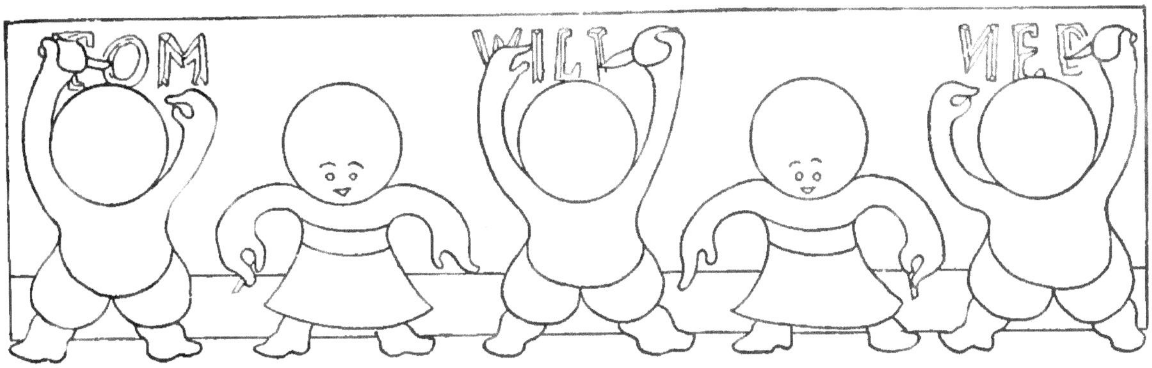

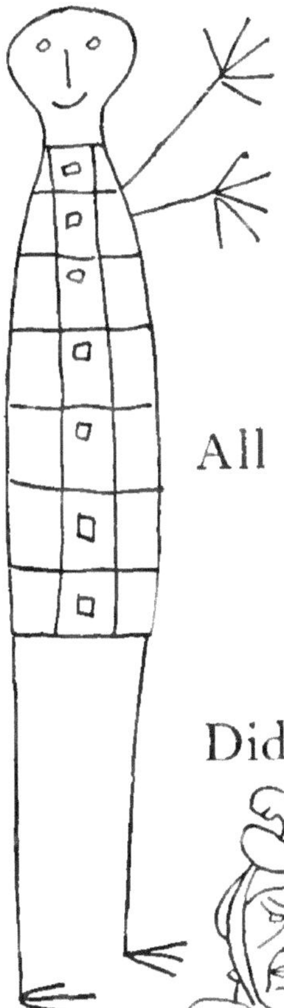

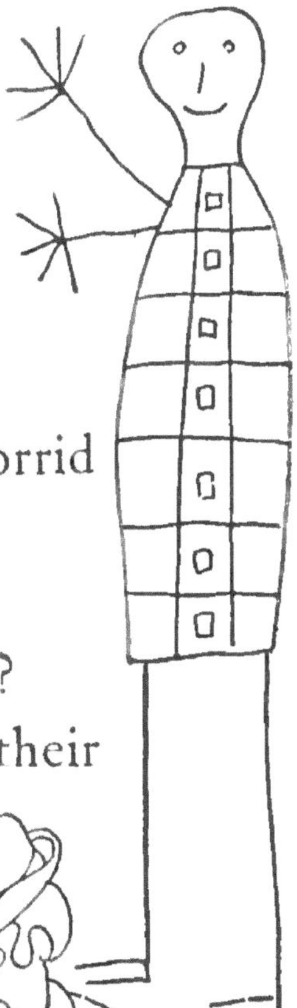

DISFIGURATION

HAVE you ever seen the scrawls
On the fences and the walls,
All the horrid little pictures and the horrid little names?
Don't you think it is a shame?
Are the Goops the ones to blame?
Did you ever catch them playing at their horrid little games?

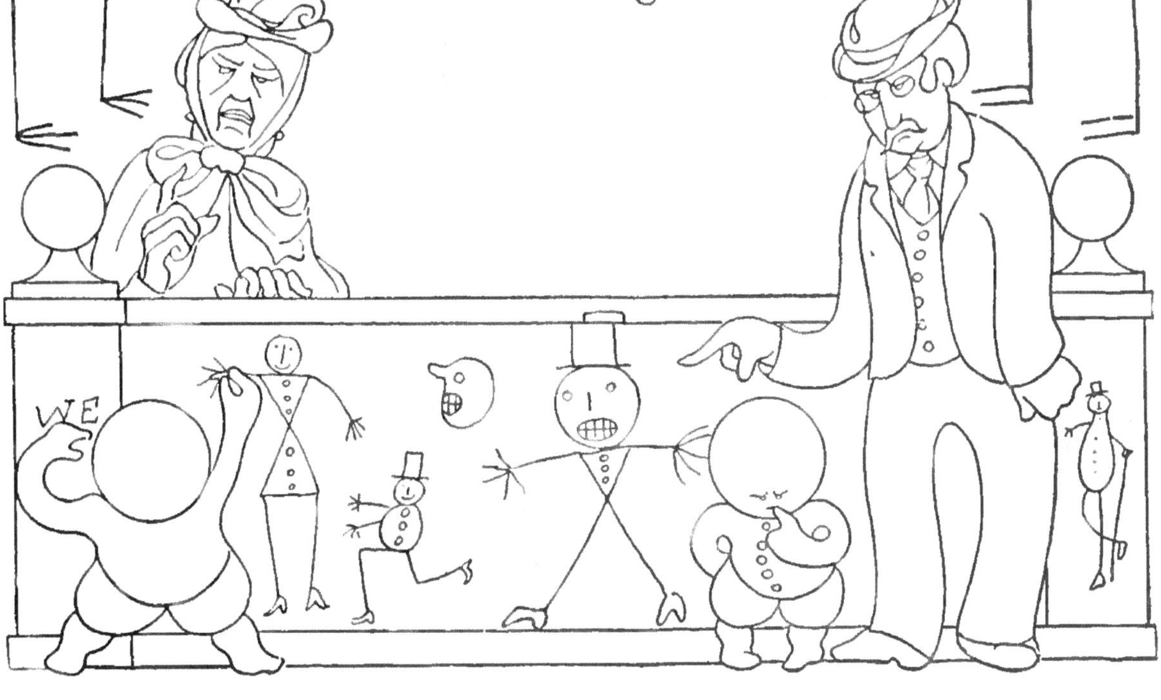
WE

BRAVERY

IT's terrible brave
To try to save
A girl on a runaway horse;
You could do that, of course!
But think of trying
To keep from crying,
When you're hungry and tired
and cross—
You couldn't do *that*,
of course!

TIDINESS

LITTLE scraps of paper,
  Little crumbs of food,
Make a room untidy,
  Everywhere they're
    strewed.

Do you sharpen pencils,
  Ever, on the floor?
What becomes of orange-
    peels
And your apple-core?

Can you blame your mother
  If she looks severe,
When she says, "It looks
    to me
As if the Goops were
    here"?

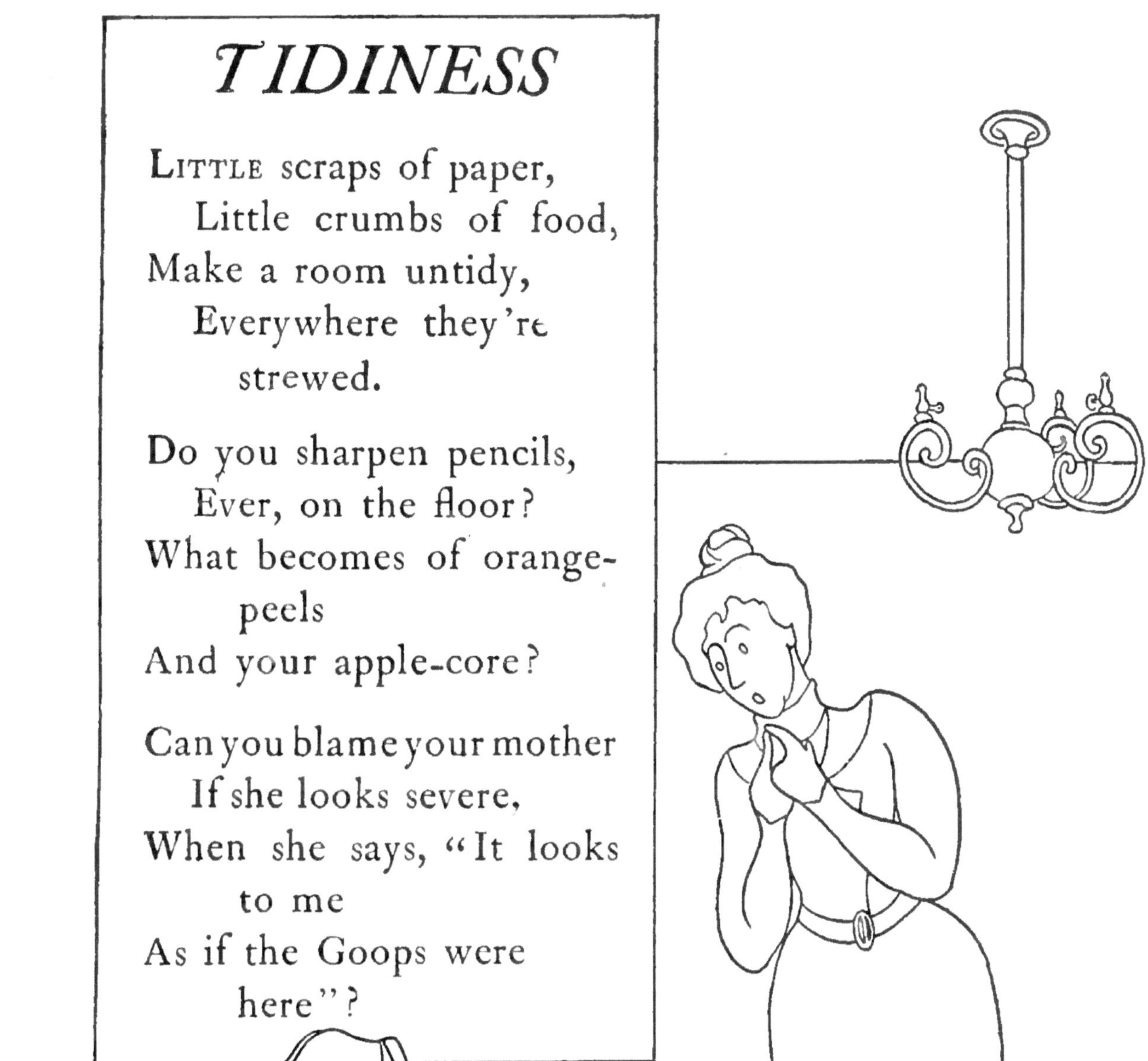

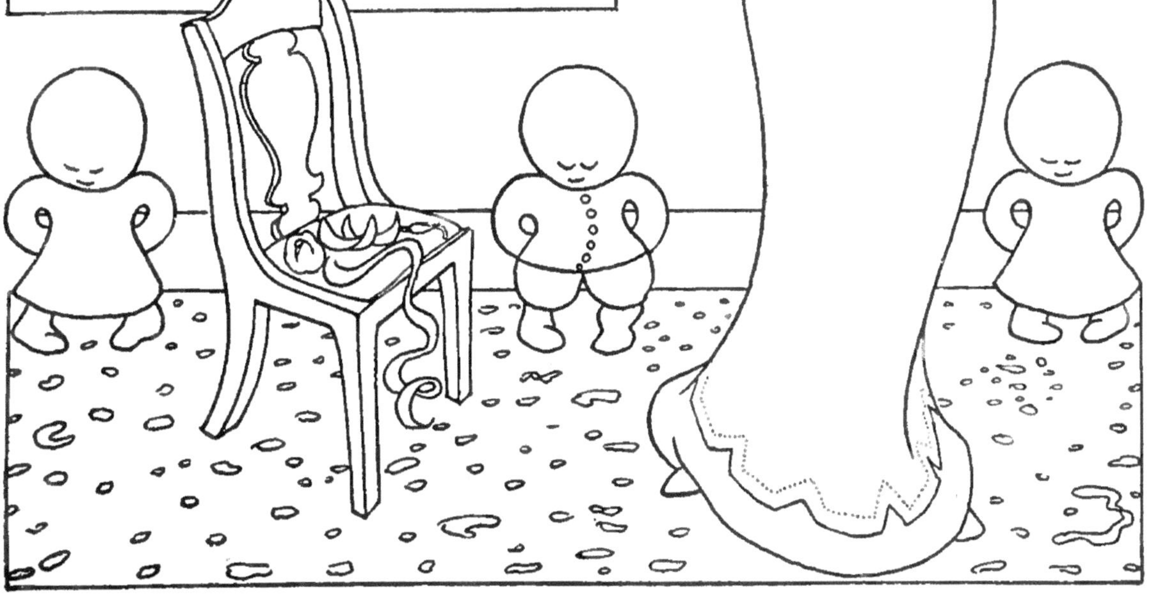

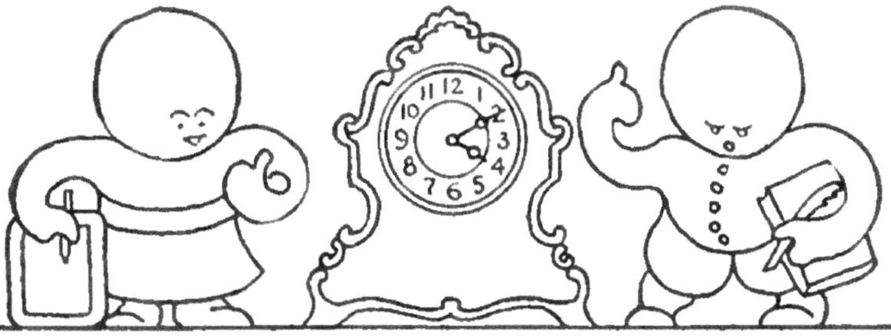

PATIENCE

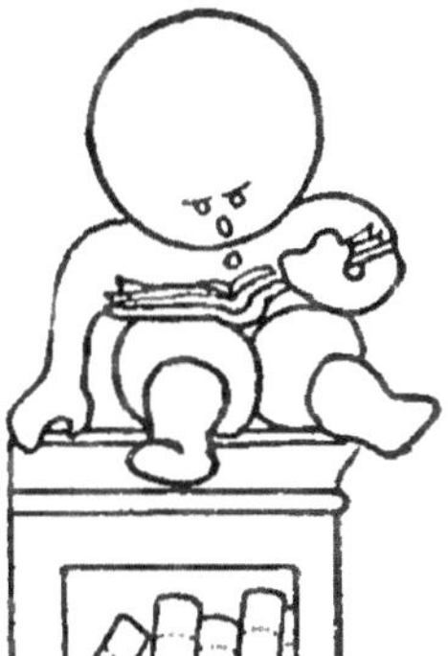

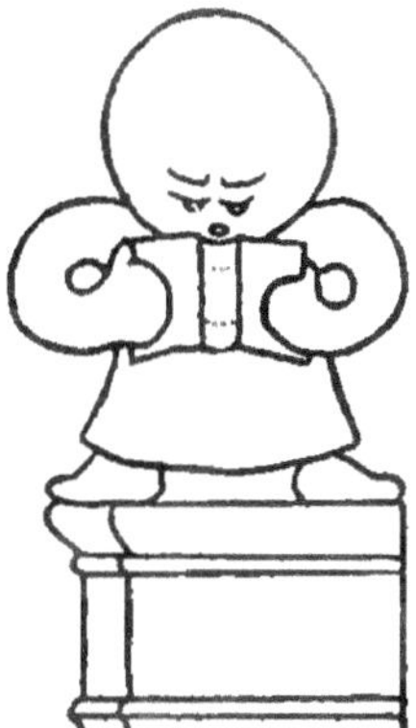

THE clock will go slow
If you watch it, you know;
You must work right along
and forget it.
So study your best
Till it's time for a rest,
The clock will go fast, if you
let it!

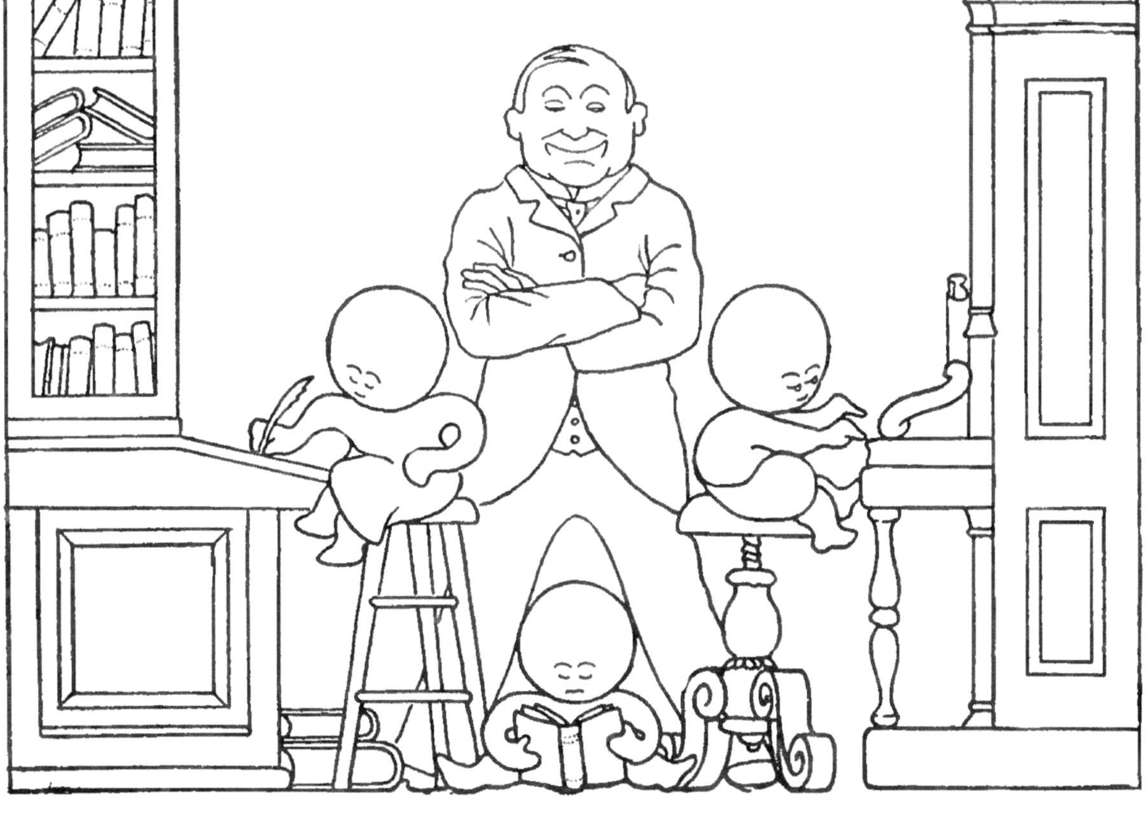

FORTITUDE

When you have been a naughty child,
    Or taken more than was your share,
When you've been sulky, cross or wild,
    You must not say, "Oh, I don't
        care!"

But when you hate to see it rain,
    And when it's time to comb your hair,
And when you have a little pain,
    Then you can say, "Oh, I don't care!"

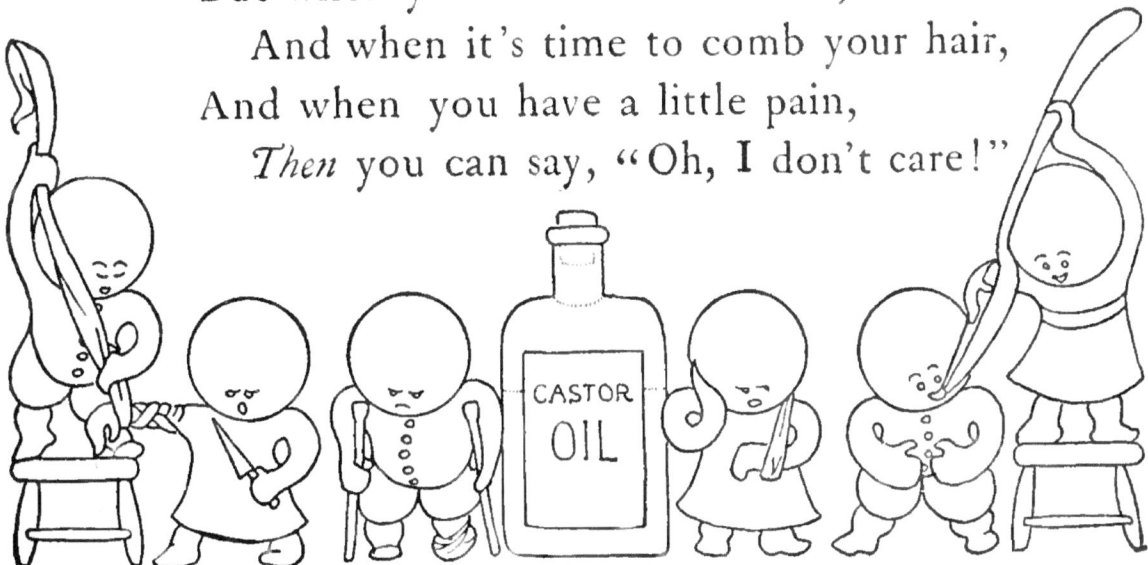

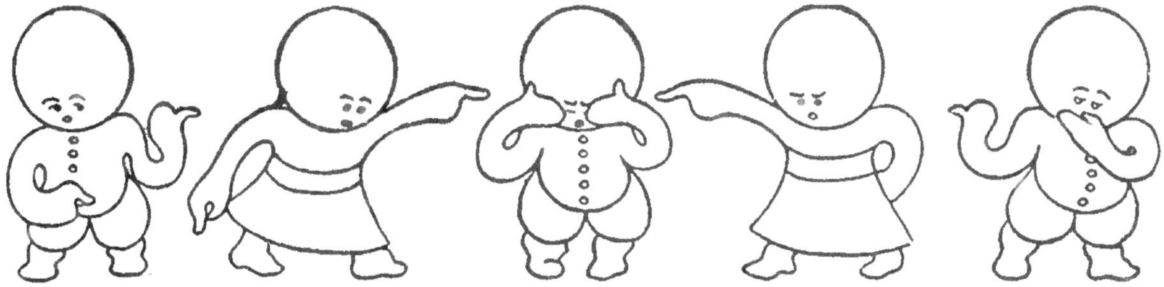

GEORGE ADOLPHUS

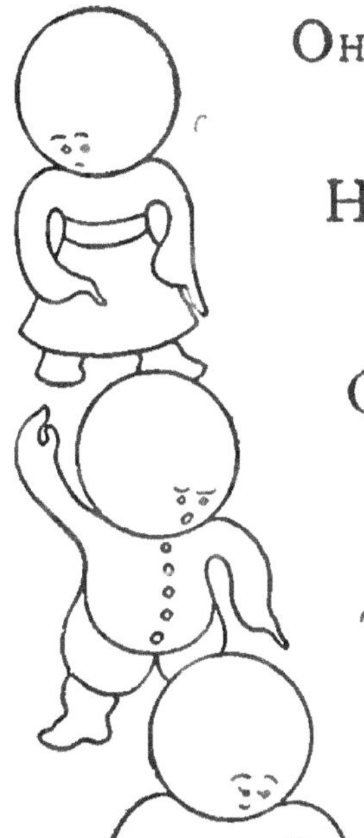

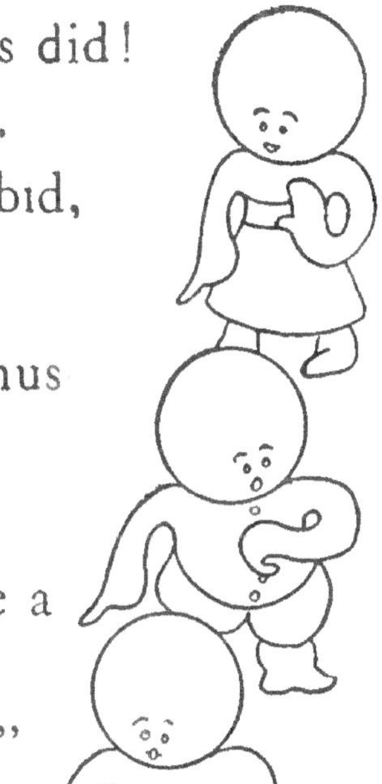

OH, think what George Adolphus did!
The children point and stare.
He went where mother had forbid,
And said he "*didn't care!*"

Oh, think what George Adolphus
did!
He made his mother cry!
The children whoop "You are a
Goop!
Fie! George Adolphus, fie!"

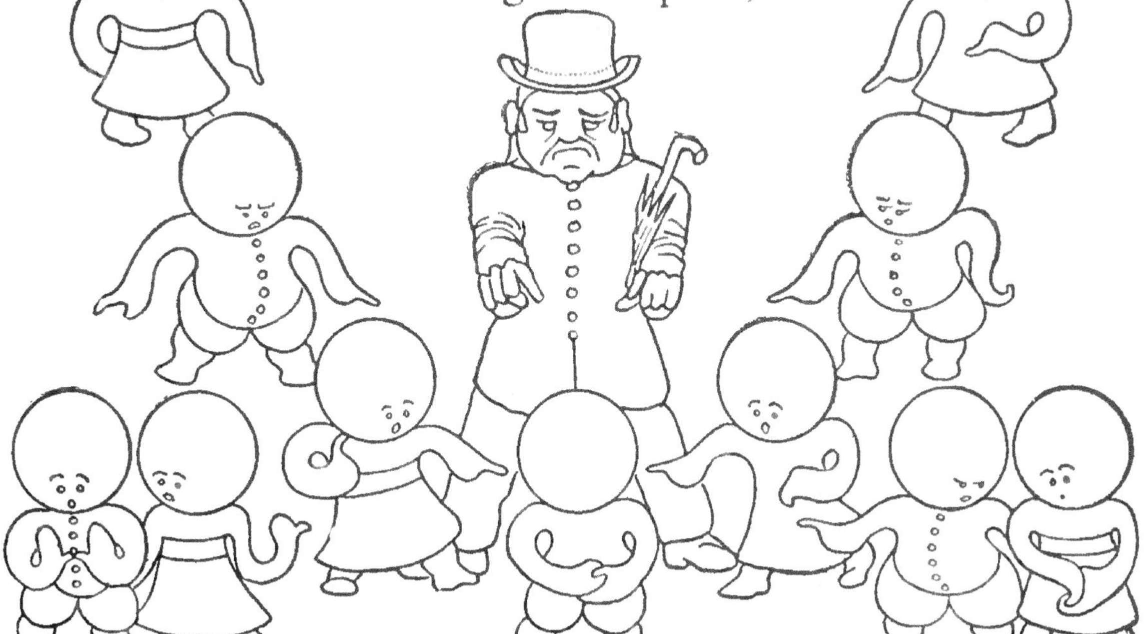

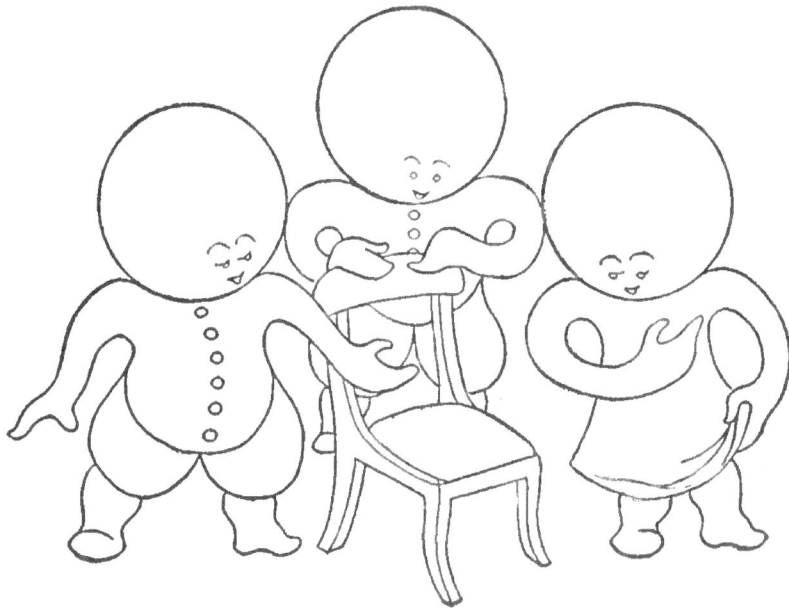

POLITENESS

I THINK it would be lots of fun
To be polite to every one;
A boy would doff his little hat,
A girl would curtsey, just like that!

And both would use such words as
    these:
"*Excuse me, Sir,*" and "*If you please;*"
Not only just at home, you know,
But everywhere that they should go.

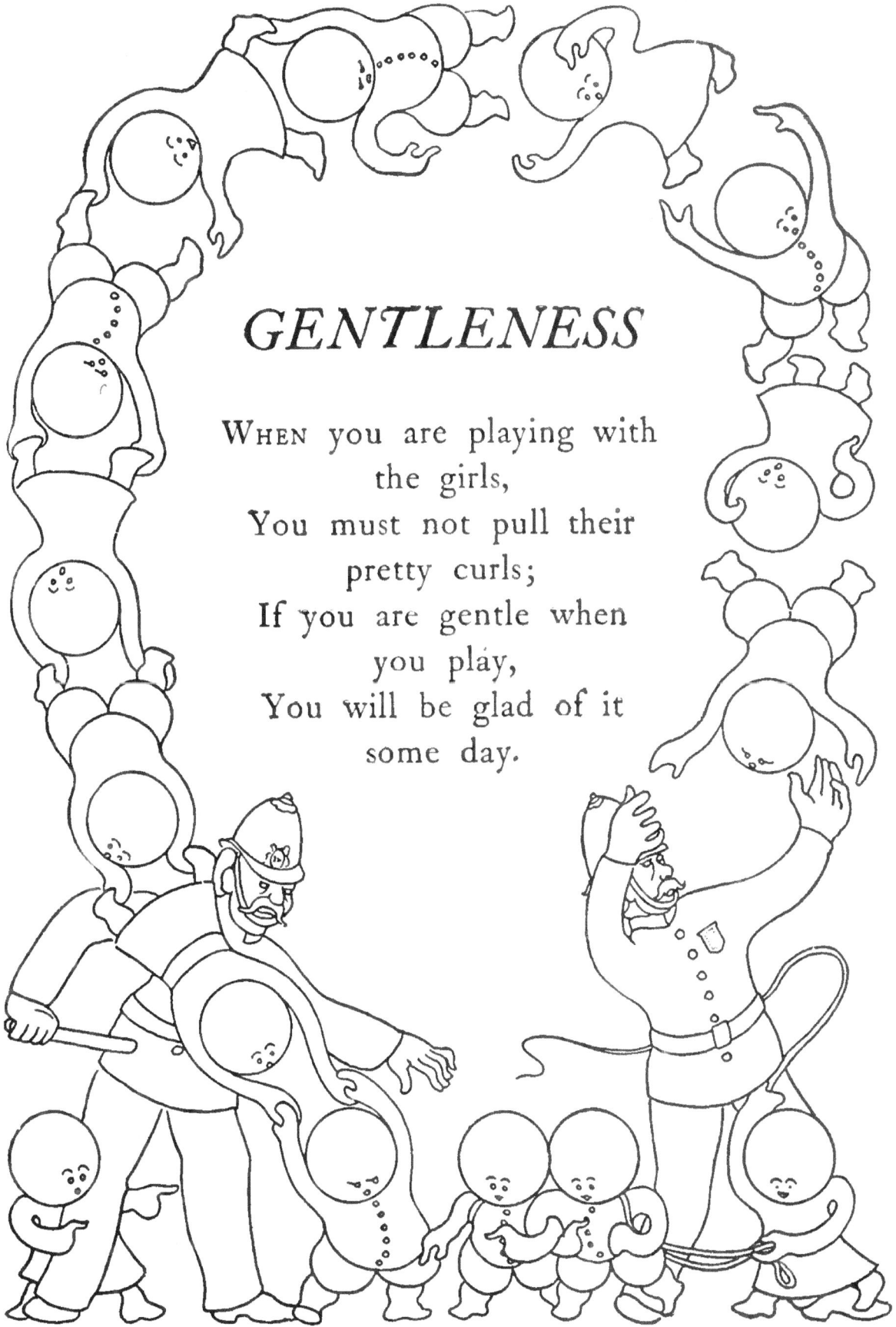

GENTLENESS

WHEN you are playing with
the girls,
You must not pull their
pretty curls;
If you are gentle when
you play,
You will be glad of it
some day.

HOSPITALITY

WHEN a person visits you, remember he's your guest,
Receive him very kindly, and be sure he has the best;
Make him very comfortable and show him all your toys,
And only play the games you're very sure that he enjoys.

When you pay a visit, never grumble or complain,
Try to be so affable they'll want you there again;
Don't forget the older ones, your hostess least of all,
When you're leaving tell her you have had a pleasant call!

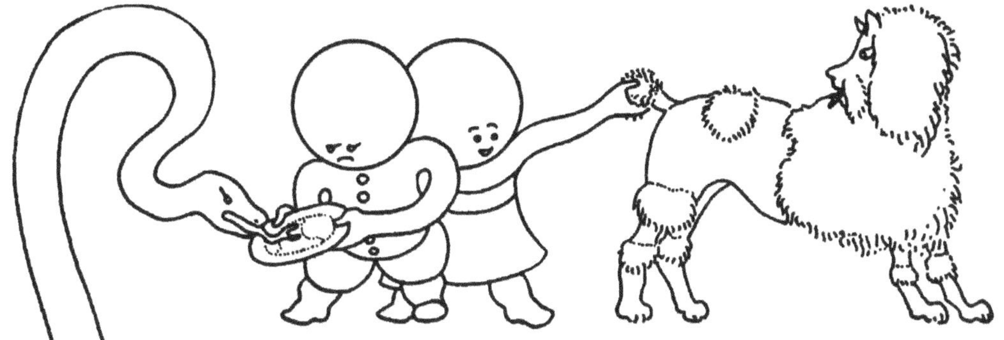

PETS

Almost every Goop forgets
When it's time to feed his pets,
'Cause his memory fails;

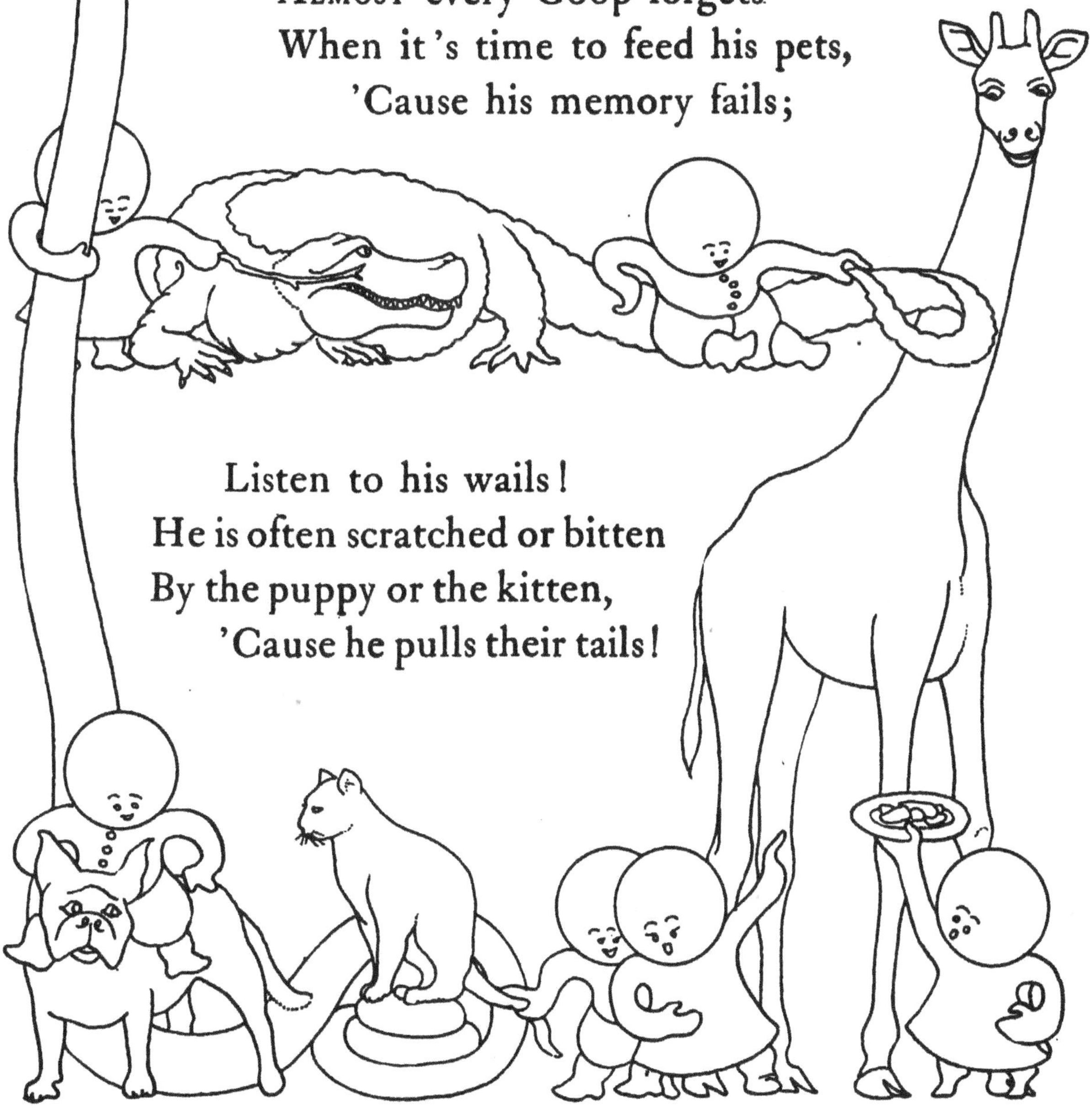

Listen to his wails!
He is often scratched or bitten
By the puppy or the kitten,
'Cause he pulls their tails!

REMEMBER

REMEMBER not to suck your thumb;
Remember not to slam the door;
Remember when the callers come
To take your toys from off the floor.

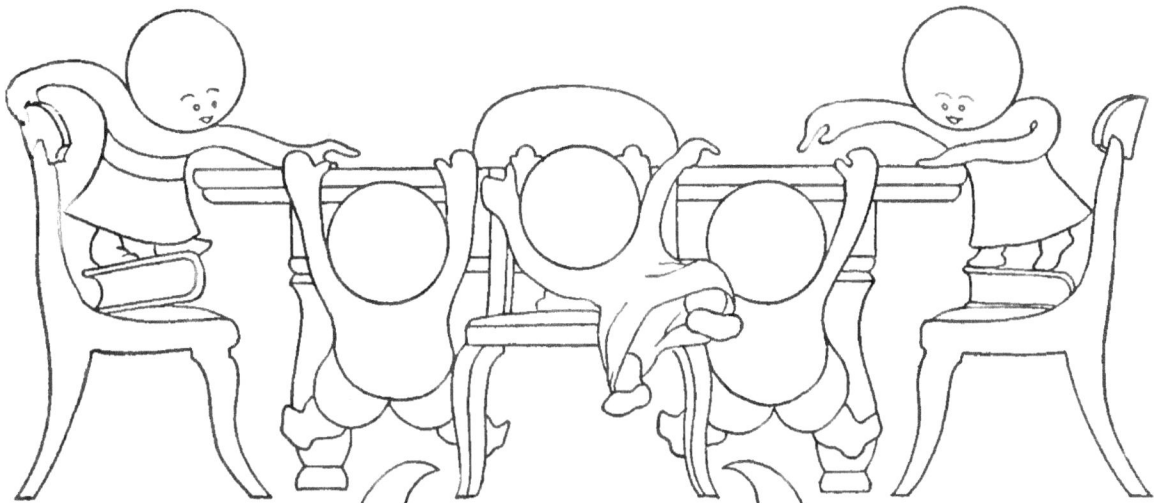

CURIOSITY

I THINK that it would help you much
If you'd remember *not to touch*.
The Goops do this, and they do more,
They peep and listen at the door!
They open bottles of cologne,
And feel of parcels not their own!
But there are many stupid folks
Who do not care for children's jokes.

PLEASE
KEEP THIS
SHUT

DO NOT
TOUCH
THIS

WILLY

WILLY broke the window-
    pane.
Willy spilled the ink,
Willy left the water-pipe
    Running in the sink!

Did his mother punish him?
    No! I'll tell you why.
Willy, he owned up to it,
    And didn't tell a lie!

Willy told his mother
    Before she found it out
He said: "I am so sorry!"
    She said "I have no doubt!

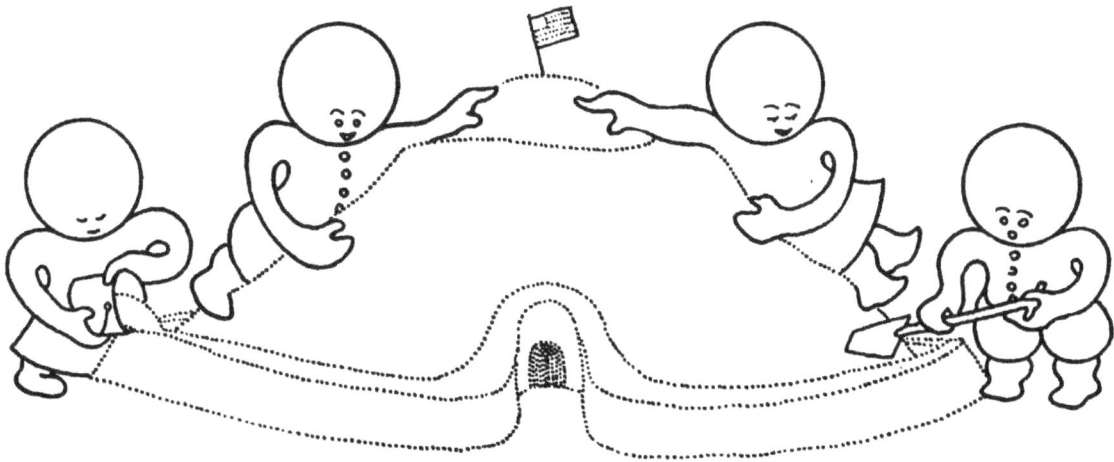

CLOTHES

WHEN you are playing in the dirt,
You should wear clothes you cannot hurt;
It will not matter, when they 're worn,
If they are just a *little* torn.

But when you 're really nicely dressed,
Be careful of your Sunday Best!
You must not crawl upon your knees;
Be careful of your elbows, please!

I
AM
NOT
VERY
DIRTY
WHILST
PLAYING

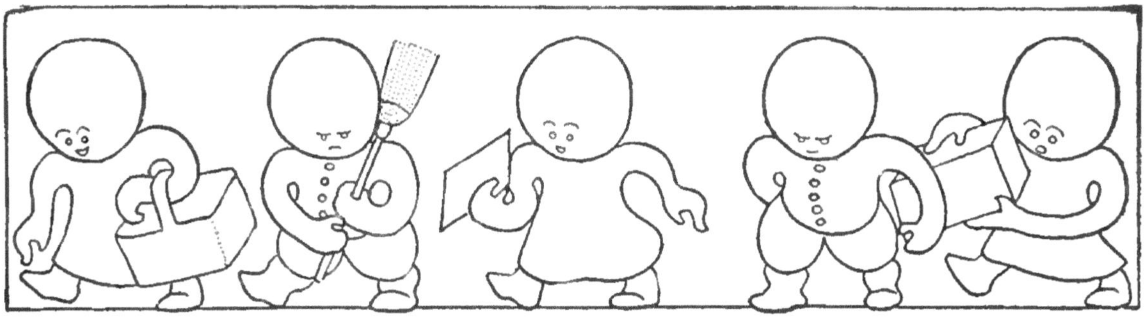

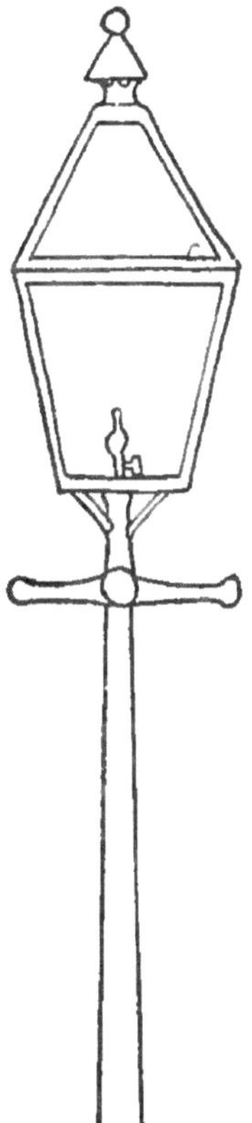

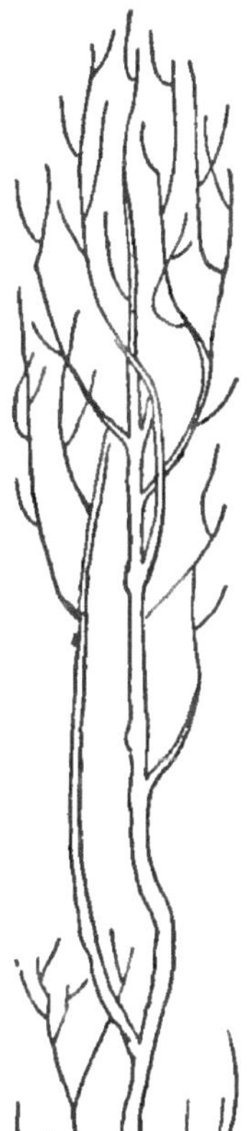

HELPFULNESS

I NEVER knew a Goop to help his mother,
I never knew a Goop to help his dad,
And they never do a thing for one
another;
They are actually, absolutely bad!

If you ask a Goop to go and post a letter,
Or to run upon an errand, *how* they act!
But somehow I imagine you are better,
And you *try* to go, and *cry* to go, in fact!

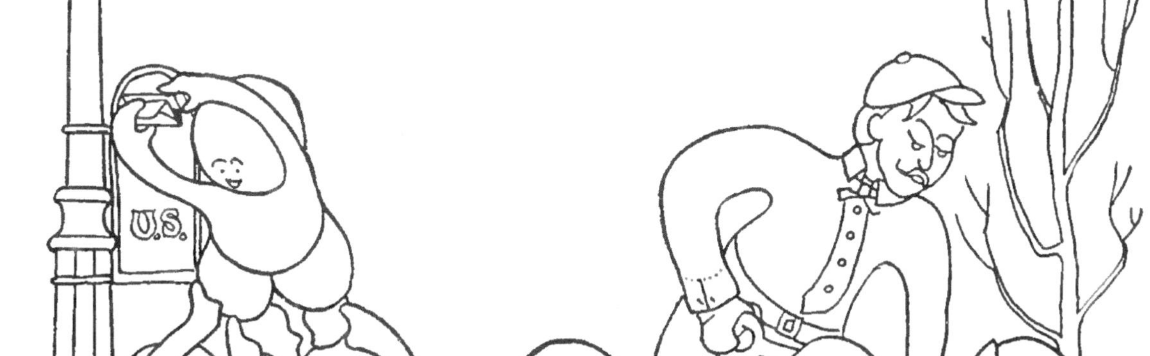
U.S.

QUIETNESS

Hush! for your father is reading.
Hush! for your mother is ill.
    Hush! for the baby
    Is sleeping, and may be
He'll catch a nice dream if you're still.
Kiss me, and promise you will!

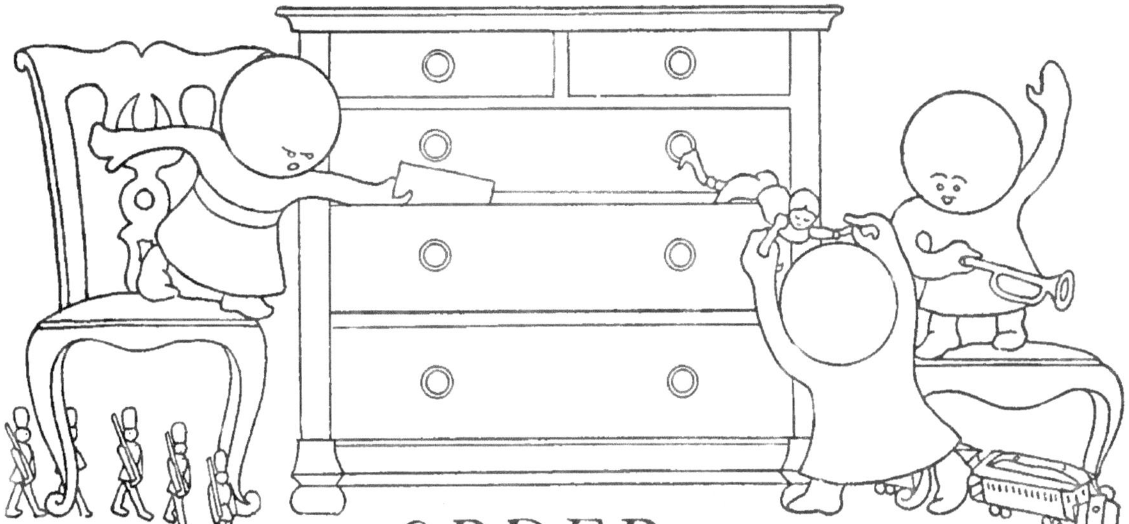

ORDER

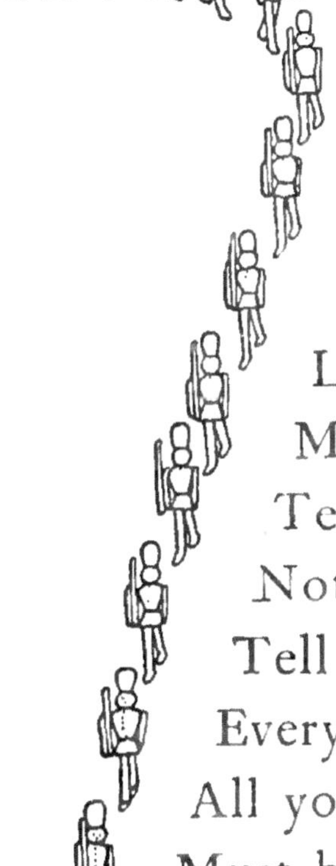

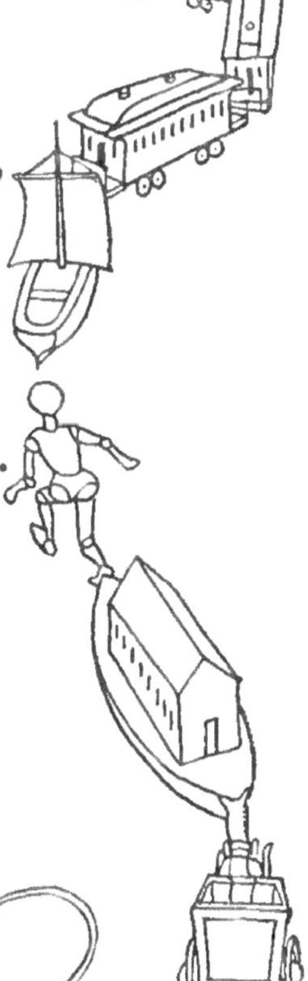

MAKE your soldiers march away,
When you 're finished with your
play.
Lead them to the barrack-box,
Make them carry all your blocks.
Teach your doll to go to bed,
Not to lie about instead;
Tell her she must clear away
Everything she 's used to-day.
All your playthings and your toys
Must be trained like girls and boys!

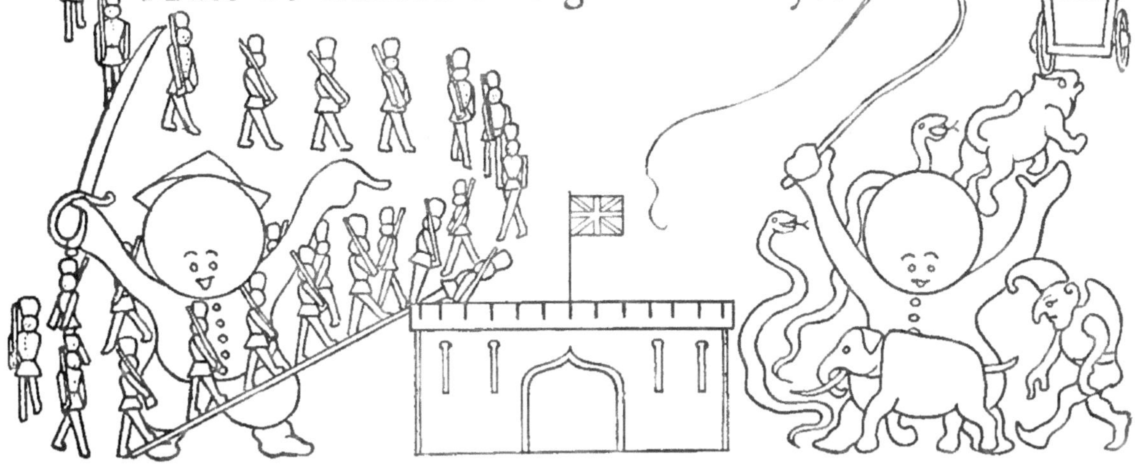

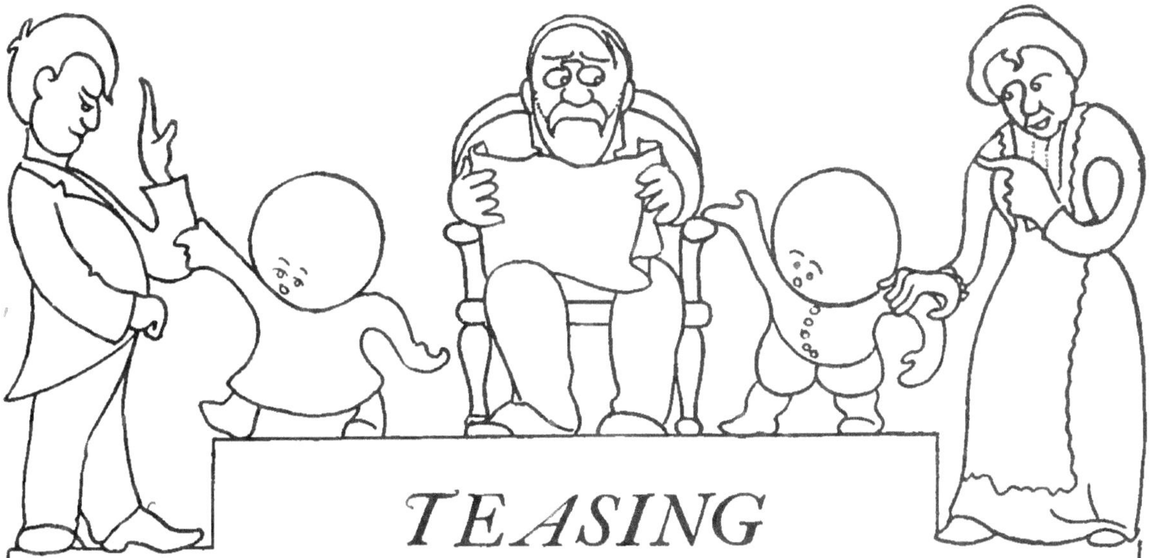

TEASING

Tease to linger longer when your mother bids you go;
Tease to have a penny when your father answers, "No!"
Tease to have a story when your uncle does n't please;
That 's the way to be a Goop—*tease, tease, tease!*

Hint about the carriage when there's only room for three;
Hint about the toys you like and every doll you see;
Hint about the candy, say you're fond
of peppermint;
That's the way to be a Goop—*hint,
hint, hint!*

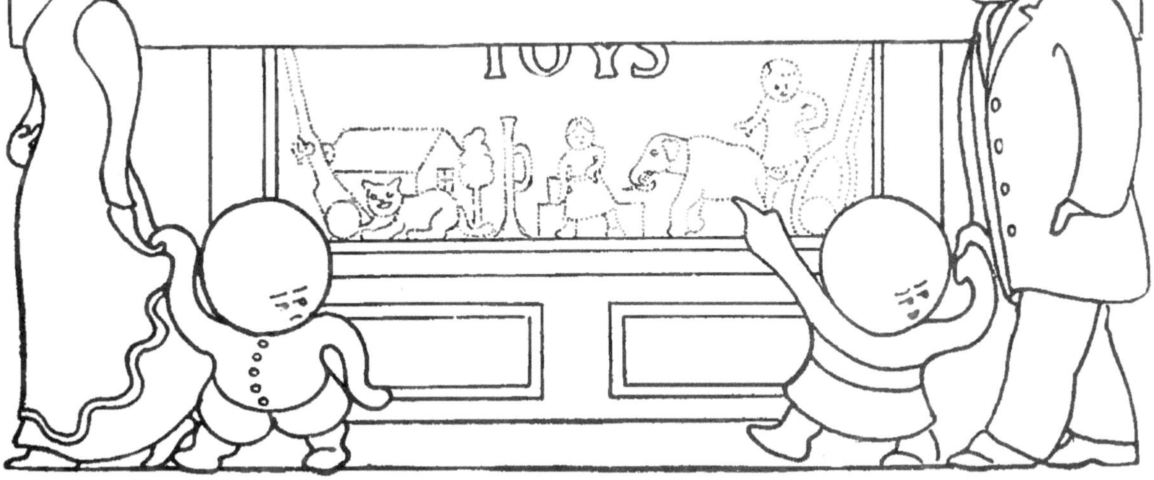
TOYS

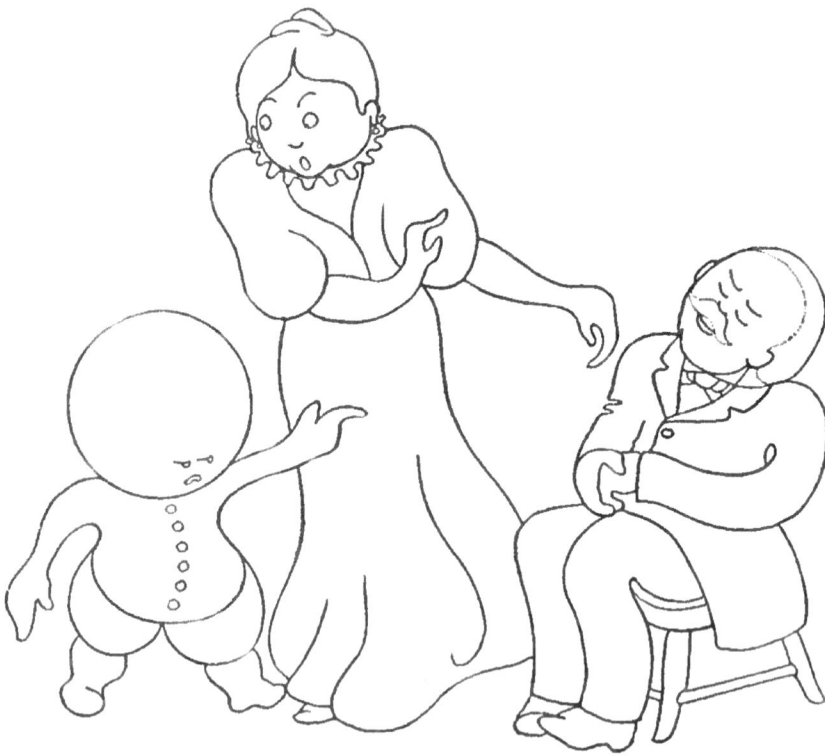

INTERRUPTION

DON'T interrupt your father when he's telling
funny jokes;
Don't interrupt your mother when she's
entertaining folks;
Don't interrupt the visitors when they have
come to call,—
In fact, it's generally wiser
not to interrupt at all.

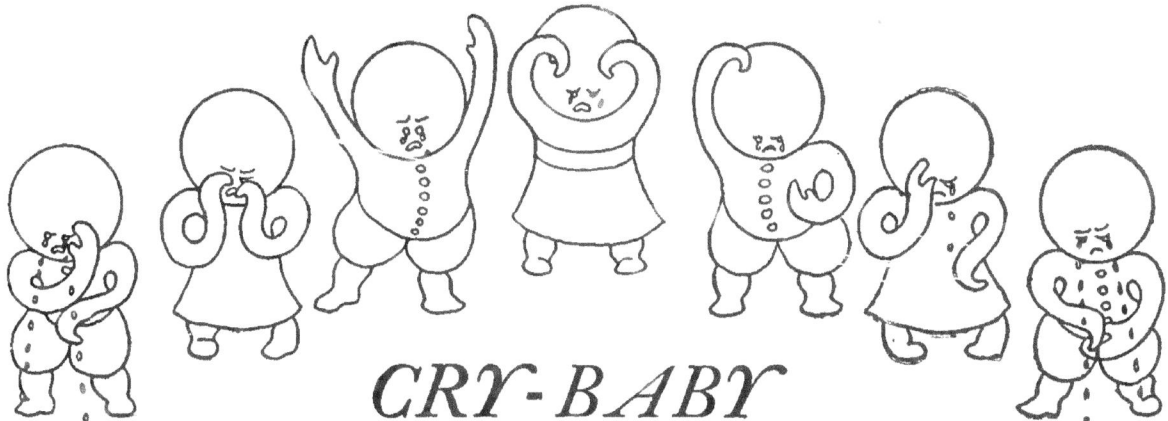

CRY-BABY

I'M sure that I would rather die
Than have my playmates see me cry;
It twists your face
And knots your forehead,
And makes you look all cross and
horrid;
And every one who sees you cries
"What *is* the matter with your
eyes?"

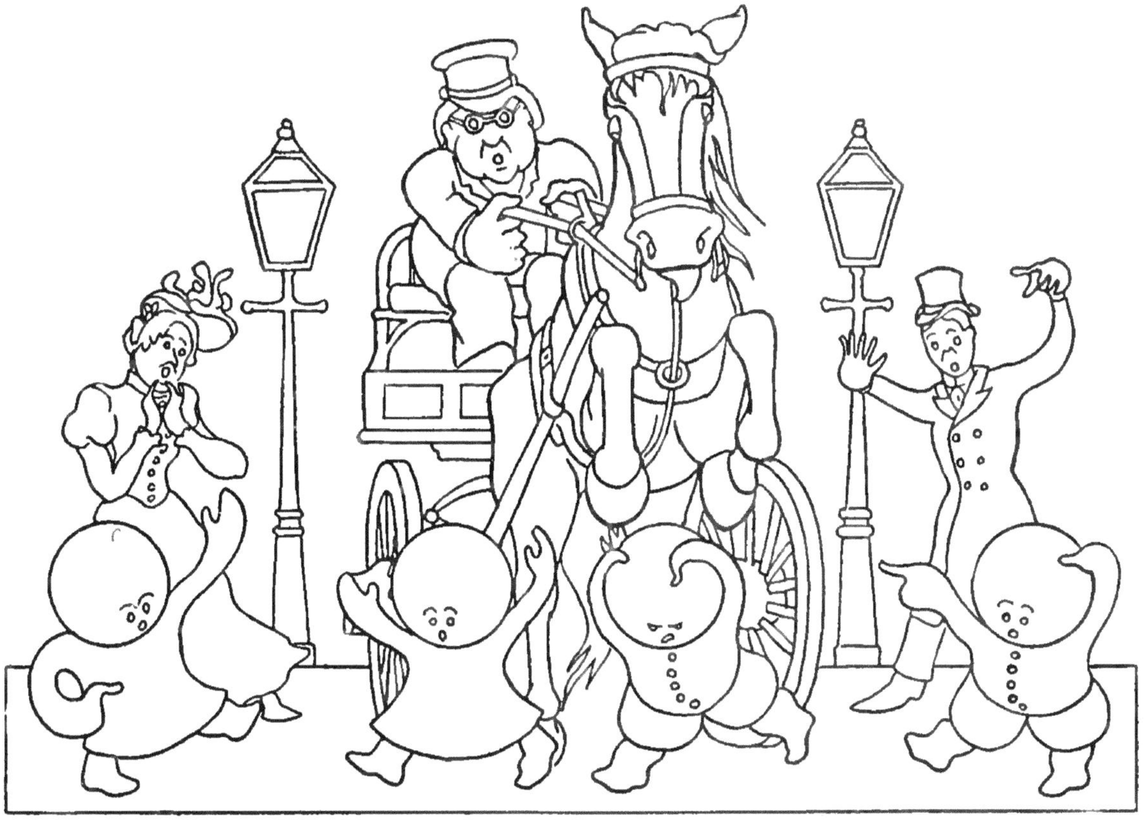

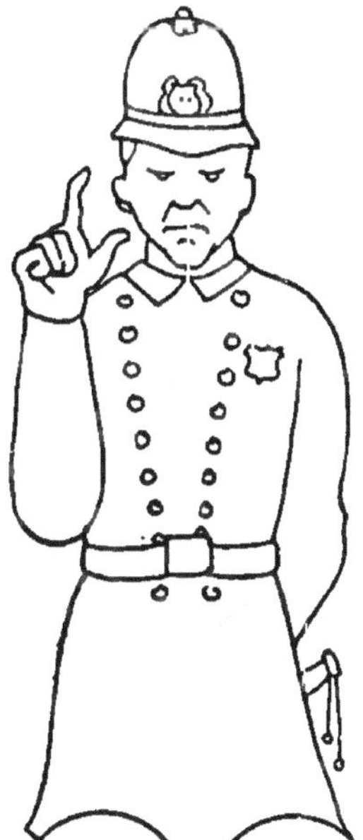

CAUTION

WHEN you travel in the street,
Are you cautious and discreet?
Do you look about for horses
When your little brother crosses?
Do you go the shortest way,
Never stopping once to play?

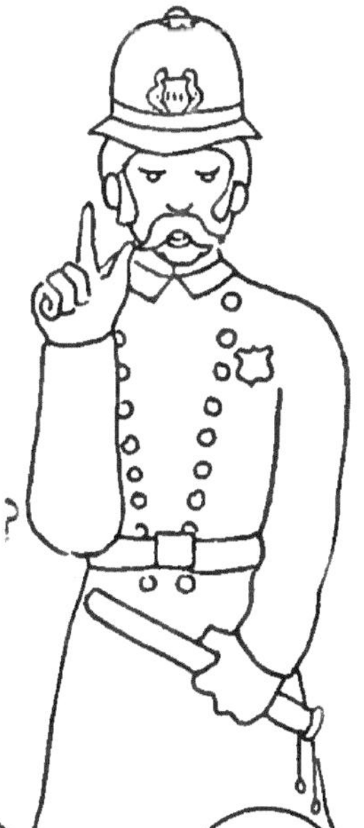

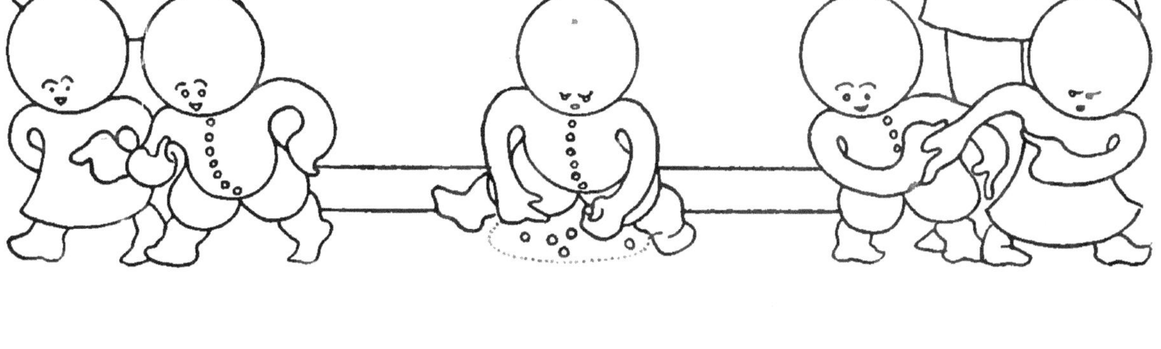

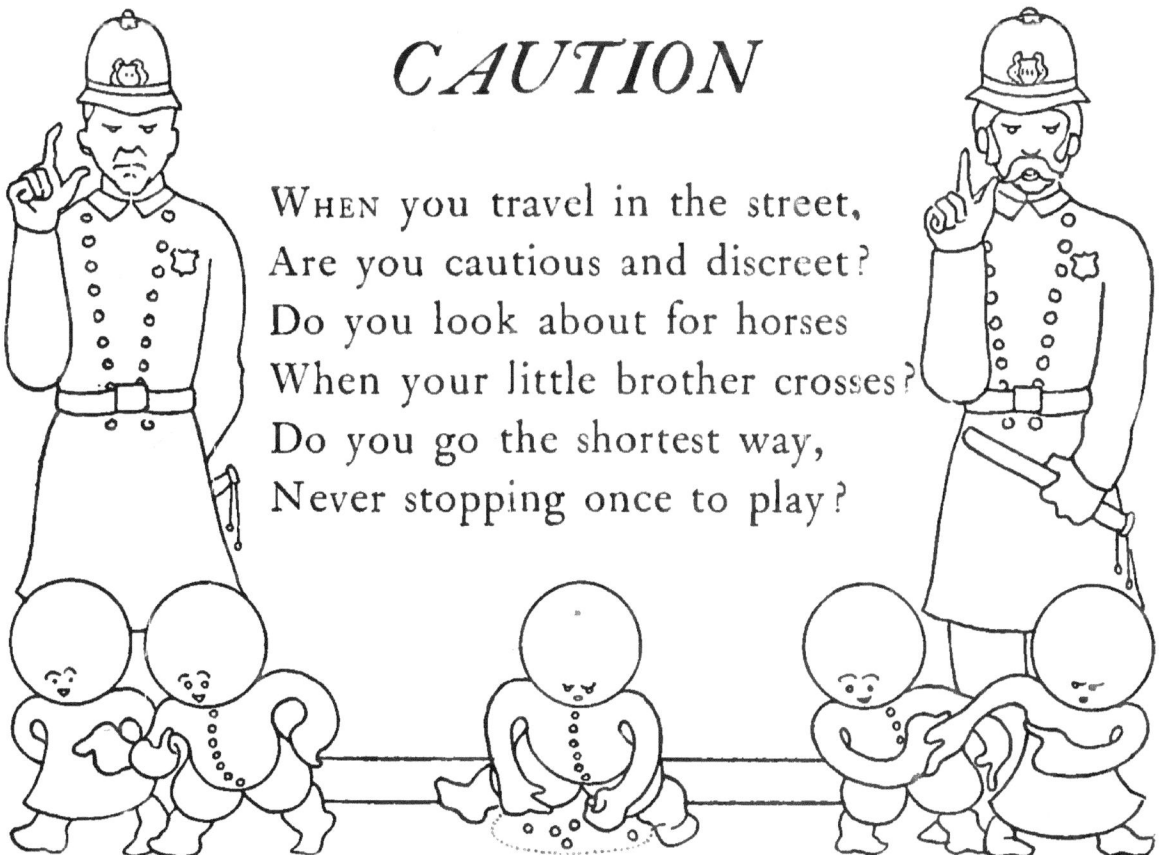

TARDINESS

GOODNESS gracious sakes alive!
Mother said, "Come home at five!"
Now the clock is striking six,
I am in a norful fix!
She will think I can't be trusted,
And she'll say that she's disgusted!

OBEDIENCE

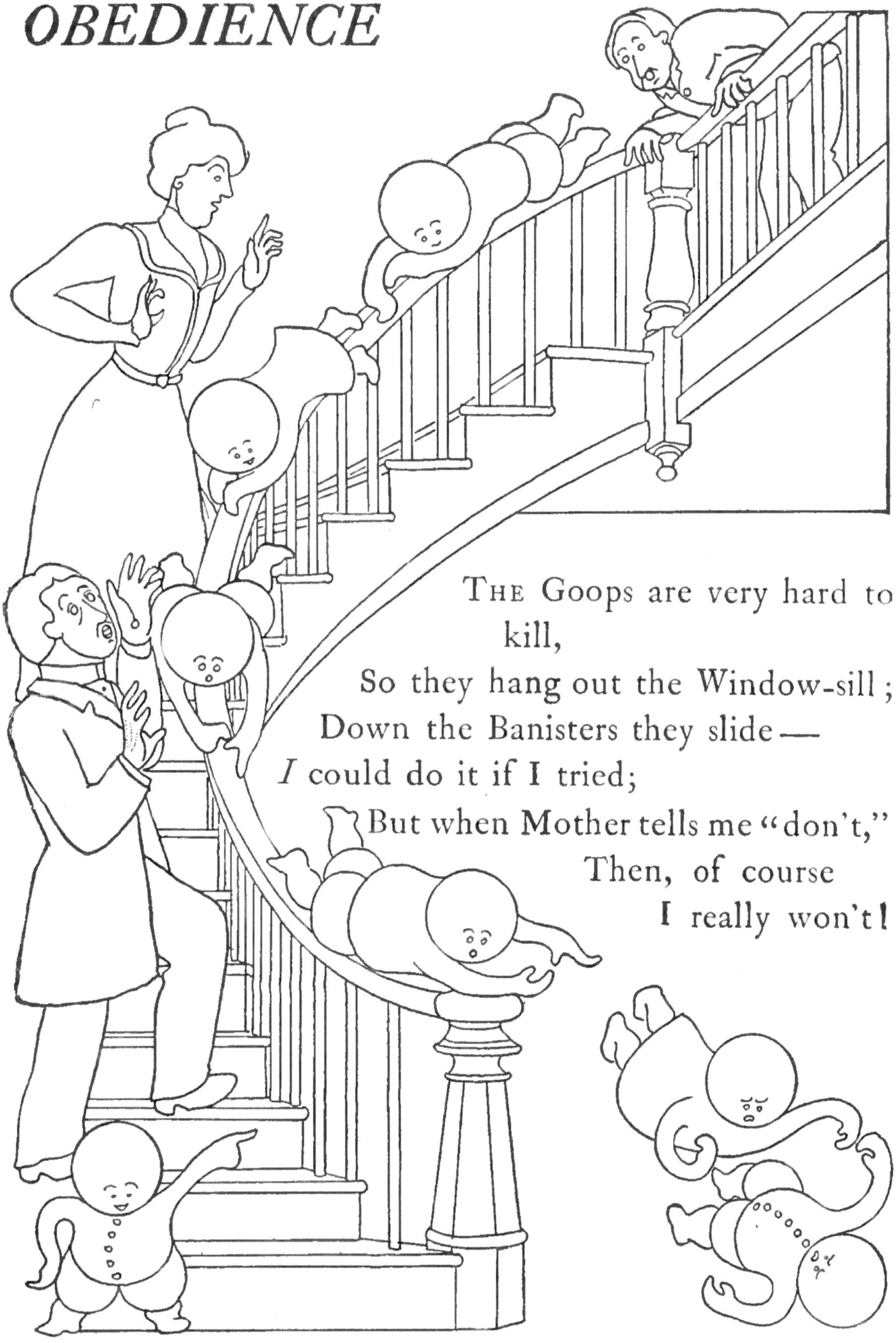

THE Goops are very hard to
kill,
So they hang out the Window-sill;
Down the Banisters they slide—
I could do it if I tried;
But when Mother tells me "don't,"
Then, of course
I really won't!

CHURCH HEADACHES

WHEN 't is time to go to church
    Do you ever have a chill?
When 't is time to go to school,
    Do you fancy you are ill?
Oh, be very cautious, please,
I can tell by signs like these
You have got the Goop Disease!

PERSEVERANCE

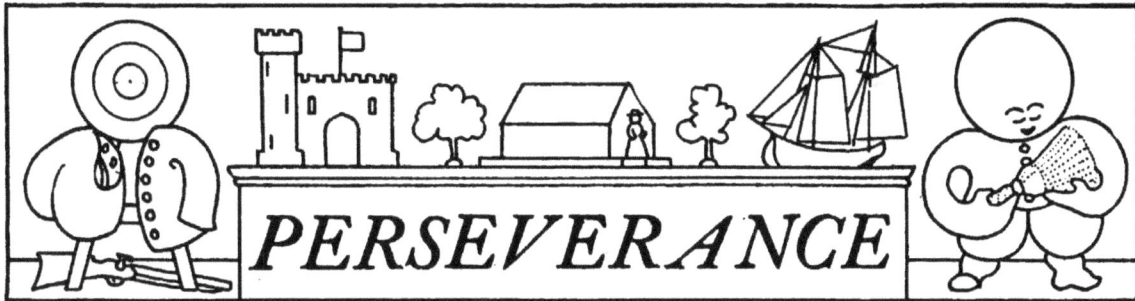

TONY started bright and early, clearing up his room,
Soon he found he had to stop and make a little broom;

So then he went into the yard to get a little stick,
But the garden needed weeding, so he set about it, quick!

Then he found his wagon he intended to repair,
So he went into the cellar for the hammer that was there;

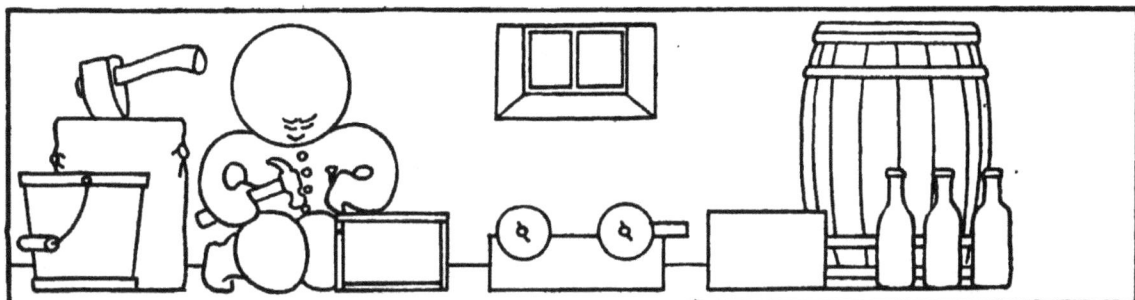

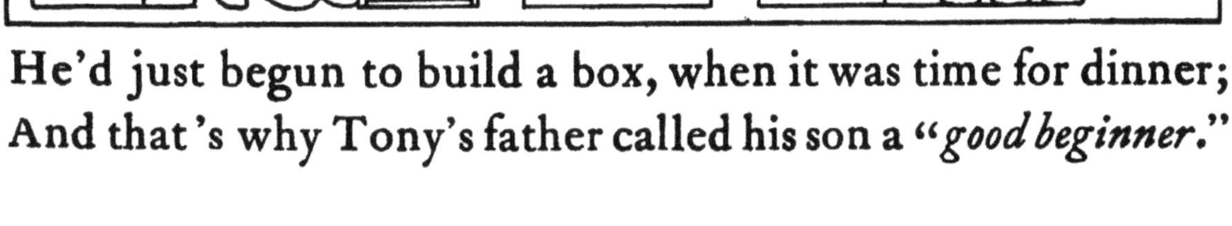

He'd just begun to build a box, when it was time for dinner;
And that's why Tony's father called his son a *"good beginner."*

DOLL-TIME

SPRING's the time for marbles
    And Fall's the time for tops,
But boys don't know, they only go
    By seeing them in shops!

They like a sled in Winter,
    In Summer 'tis a kite;
But dolls are found the whole year
      round
    And every day and night!

COMBING & CURLING

When your mother combs your hair,
Here's a rhyme for you to say:
If you try it, I declare,
It will take the snarls away!

In the ocean of my hair,
Many little waves are there;
Make the comb, a little boat,
Over all the billows float;
Sail the rough and tangled tide
Till it's smooth on every side,
Till, like other little girls,
I've a sea of wavy curls!

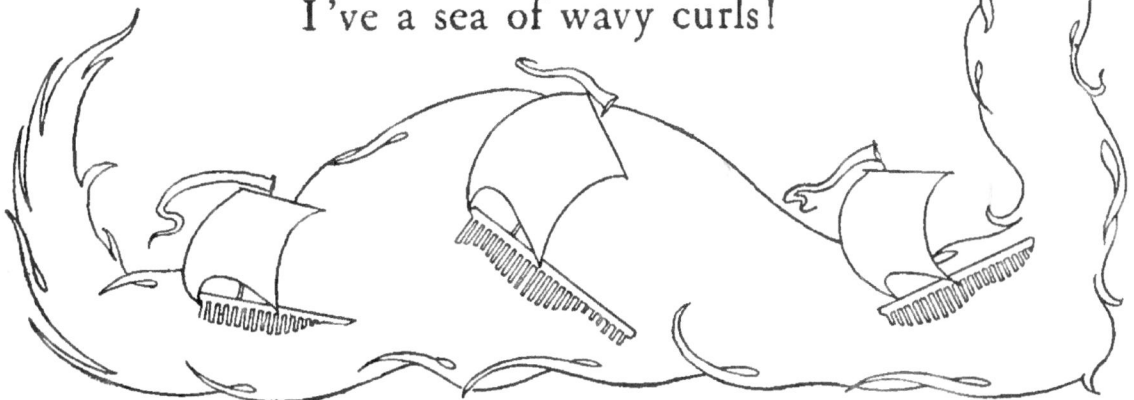

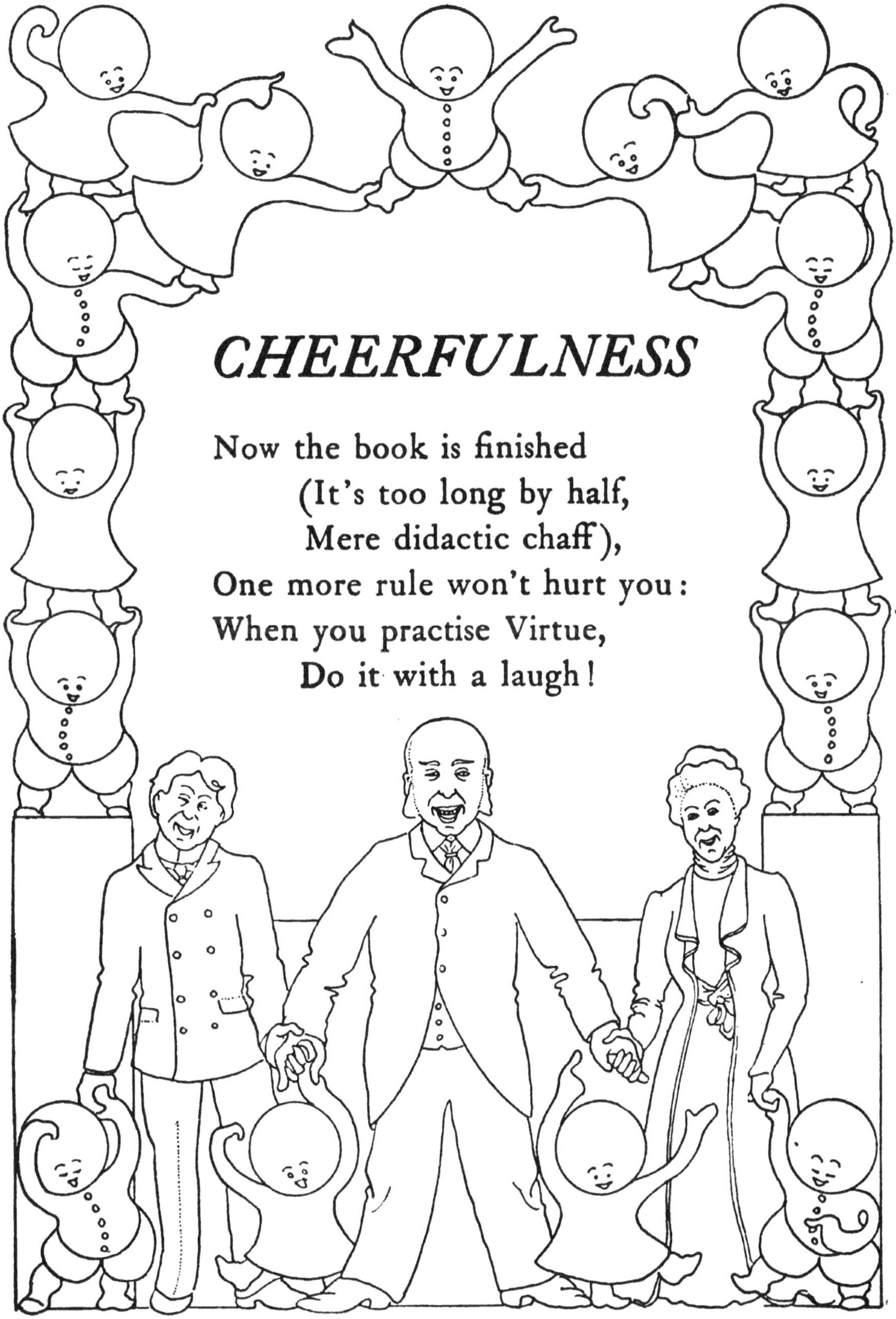

CHEERFULNESS

Now the book is finished
    (It's too long by half,
    Mere didactic chaff),
One more rule won't hurt you:
When you practise Virtue,
    Do it with a laugh!

MORE
GOOPS
AND
HOW NOT TO BE THEM

M O R E
G O O P S

AND

HOW NOT TO BE THEM

A Manual of Manners for Impolite Infants
Depicting the Characteristics of Many
Naughty and Thoughtless Children
With Instructive Illustrations

By GELETT BURGESS

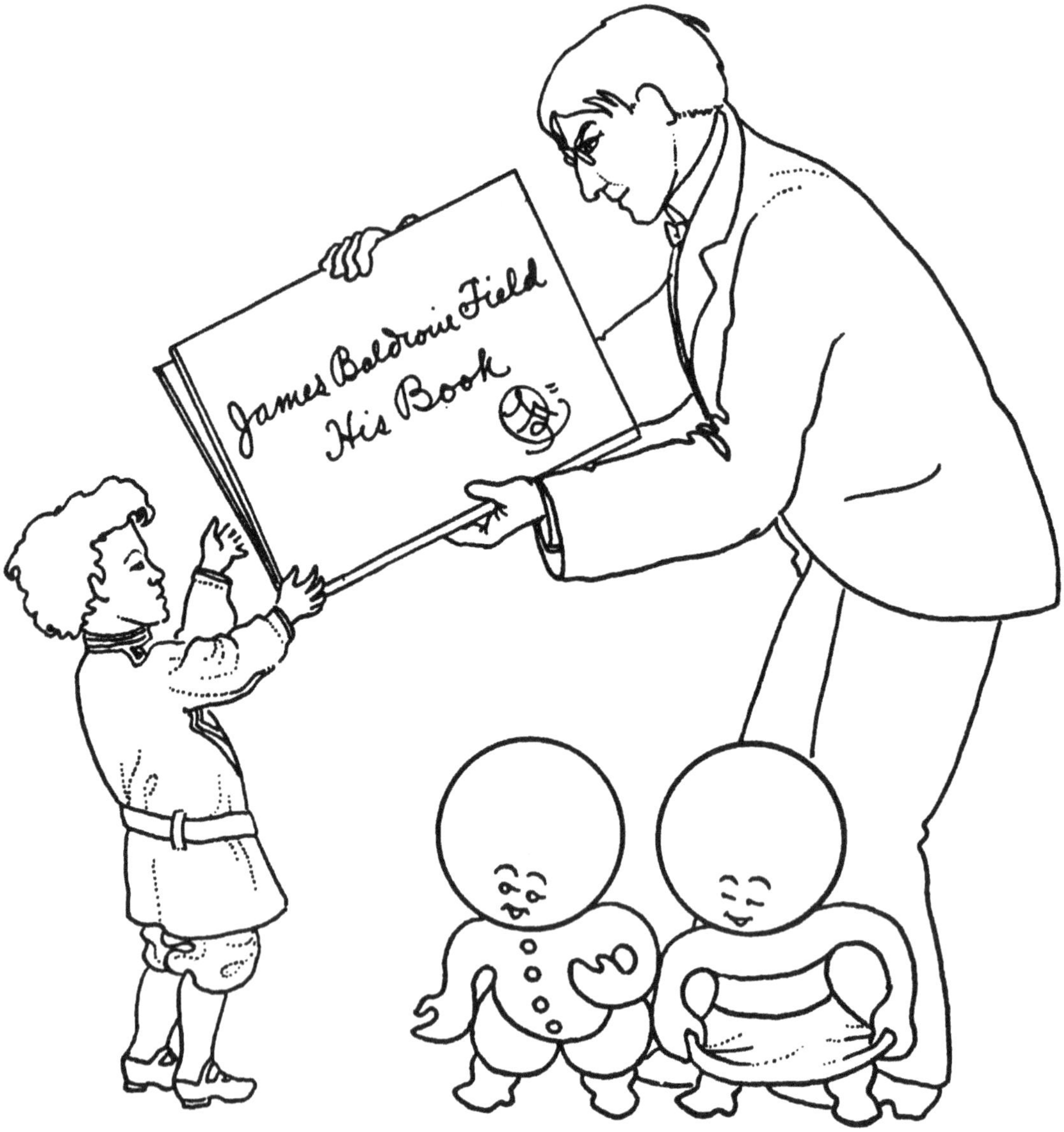
James Baldwin Field
His Book

CONTENTS

TABLE OF CONTENTS

INTRODUCTION

CHILDREN, although you might expect
My manners to be quite correct
(For since I fancy I can teach,
I ought to practice what I preach),
'T is true that I have often braved
My mother's wrath, and misbehaved!
And almost every single rule
I broke, before I went to school!
For that is how I learned the way
To teach you etiquette to-day.
So when you chance to take a look
At all the maxims in the book,
You 'll see that most of them are true,
I found them out, and so will you,
For if you are as GOOP derided,
You may perhaps reform, as I did!

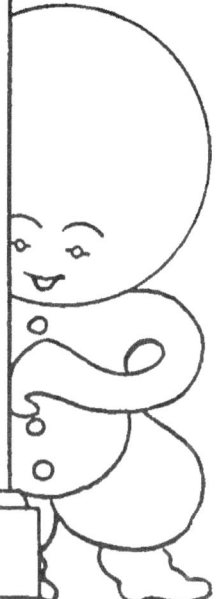

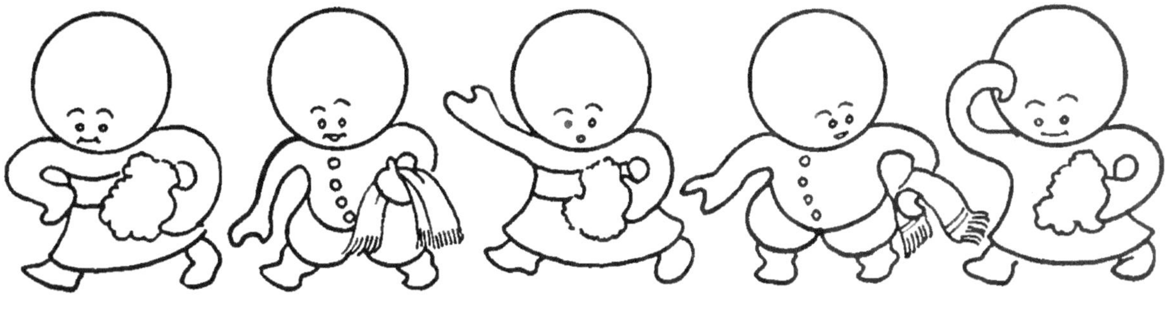

WINDOW-SMOOCHERS

LITTLE Goops are marking
On the window pane;
I forbid, in vain!
Noses, when they're greasy,
Leave a smooch so easy!
Rub it out again!
I shall have to scold them,
For I've often told them,
Kindly, to refrain!

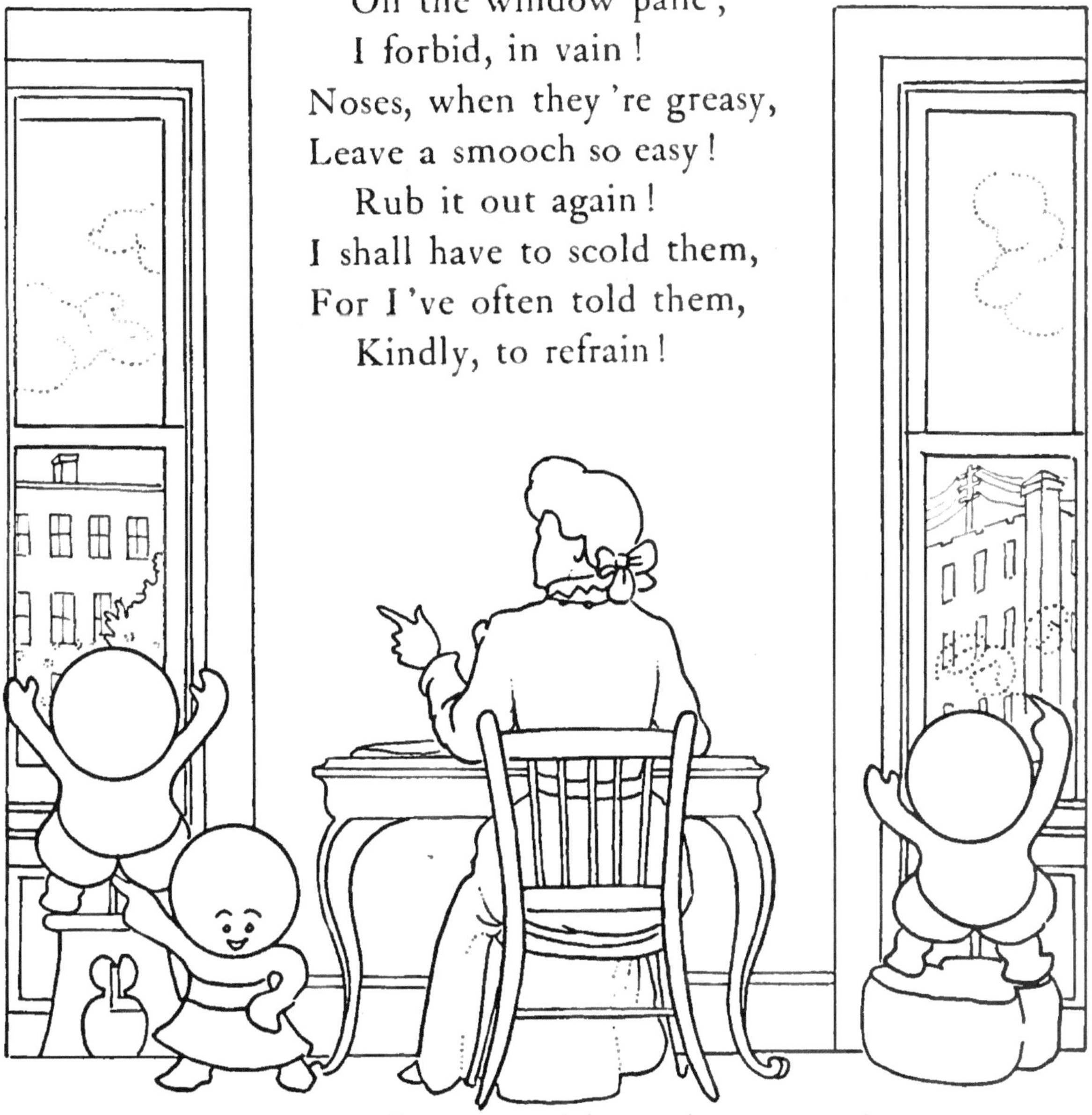

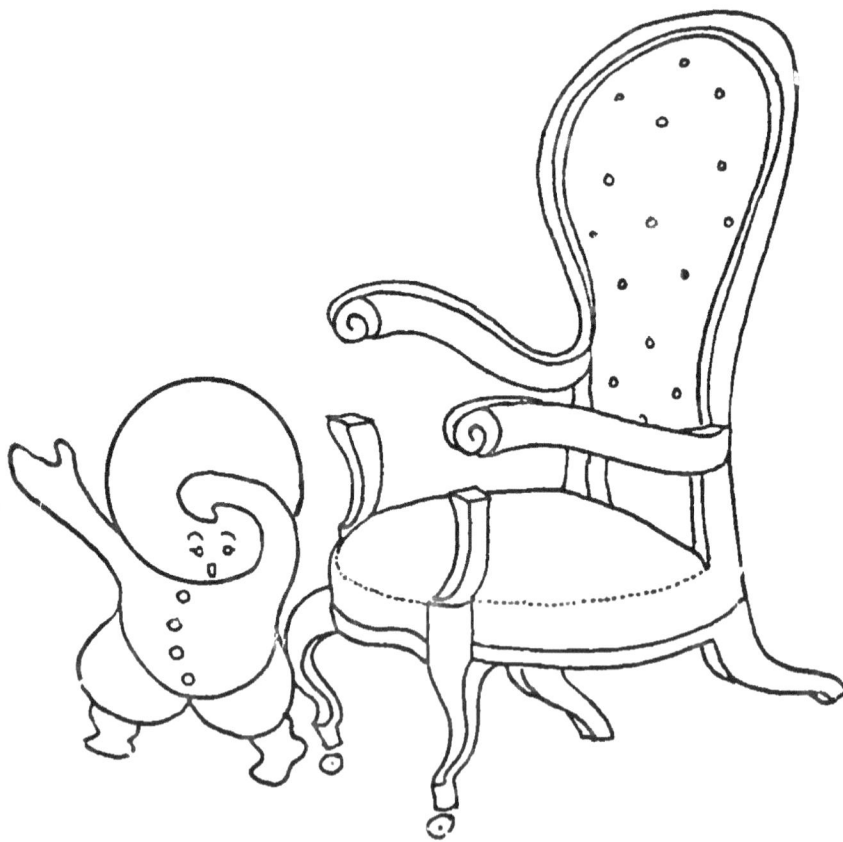

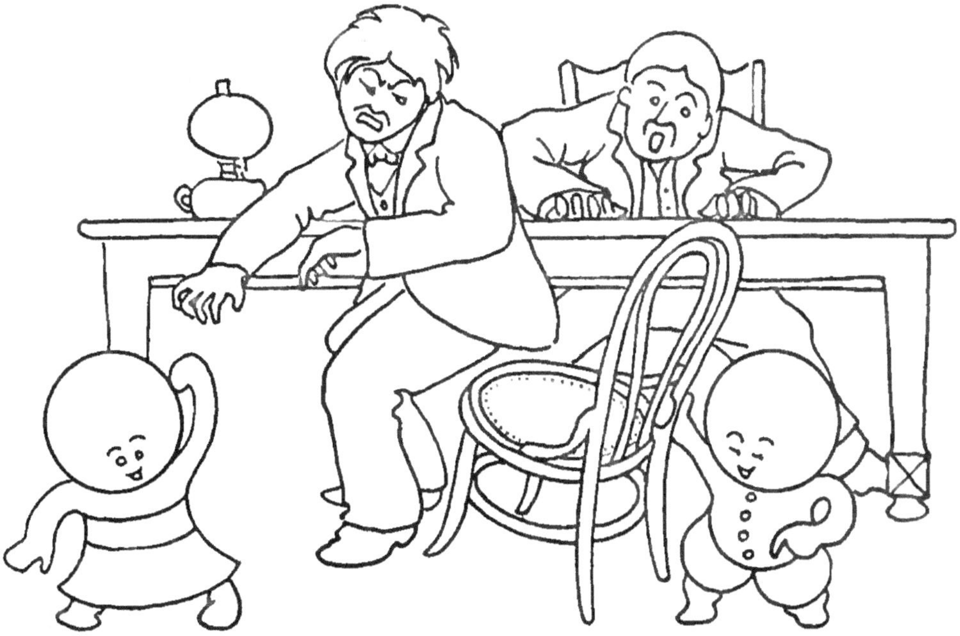

A LOW TRICK

THE meanest trick I ever knew
Was one I know *you* never do.
I saw a Goop once try to do it,
And there was nothing funny to it.
He pulled a chair from under me
As I was sitting down; but he
Was sent to bed, and rightly, too.
It was a *horrid* thing to do!

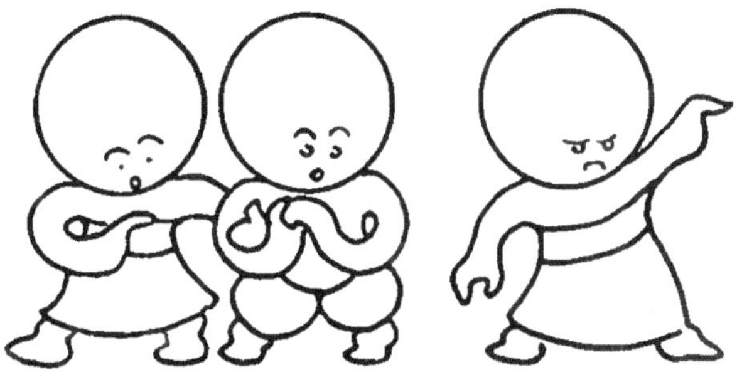

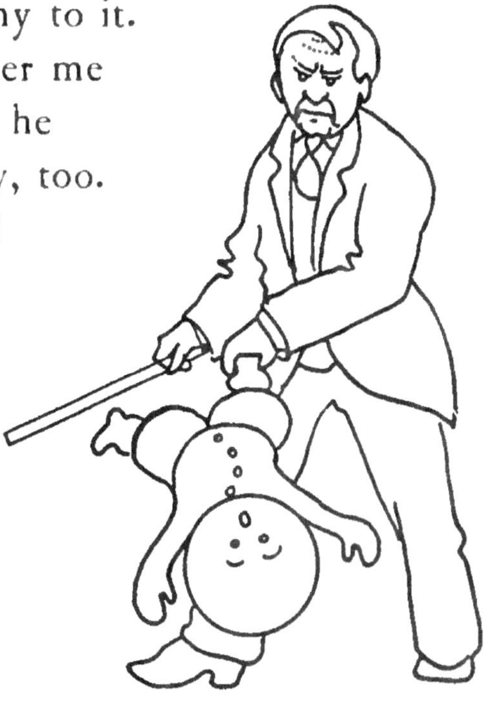

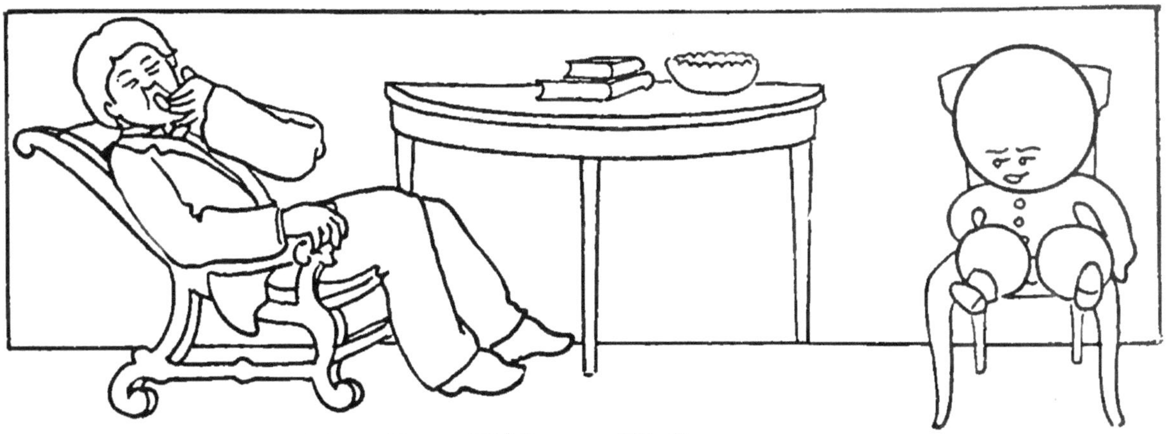

WHEN TO GO

WHEN you go a-calling,
  Never stay too late;
You will wear your welcome out
  If you hesitate!
Just before they're tired of you,
  Just before they yawn,
Before they think you are a Goop,
  And wish that you were gone,
While they're laughing with you,
  While they like you so,
While they want to keep you,—
  That's the time to go!

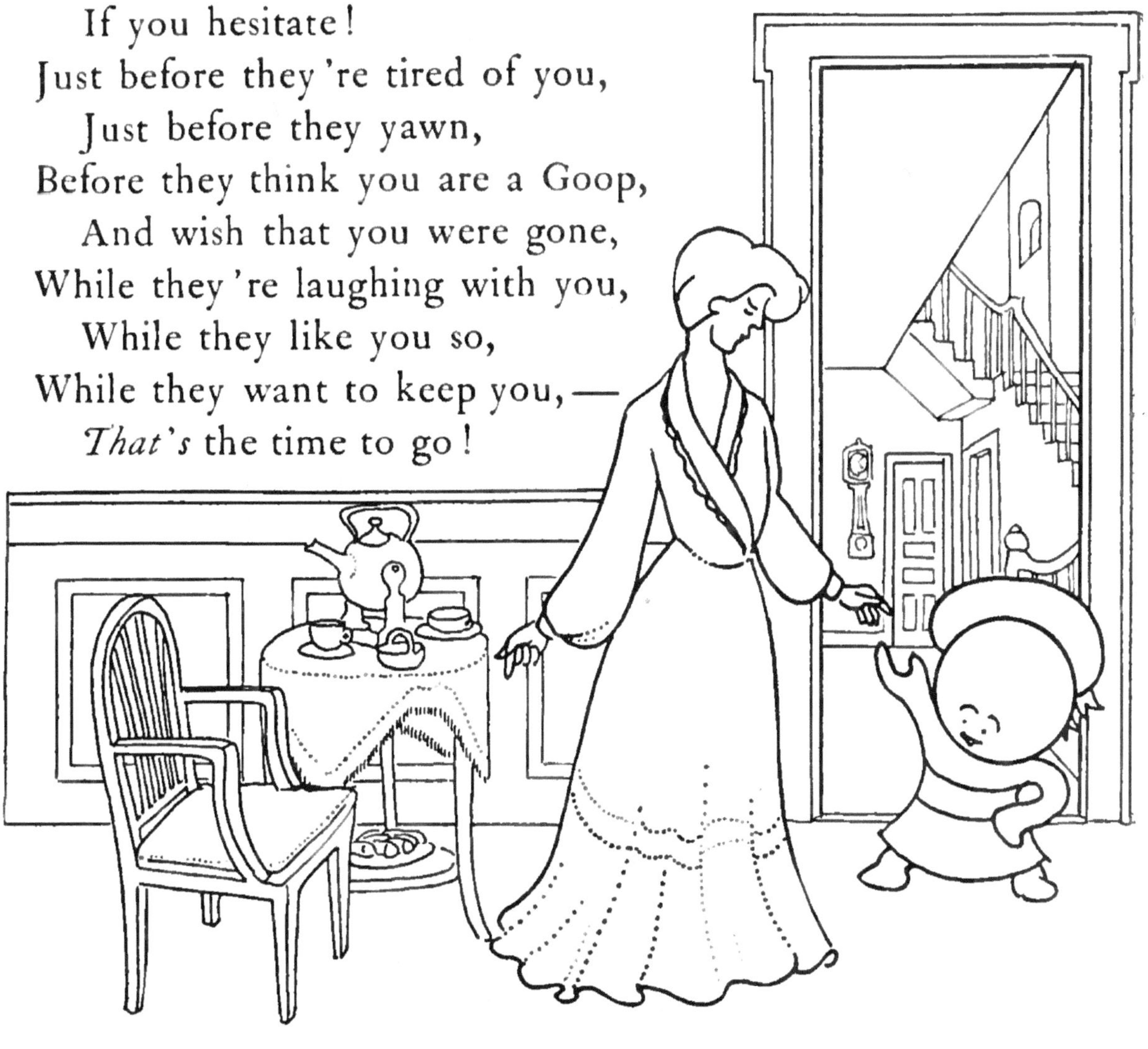

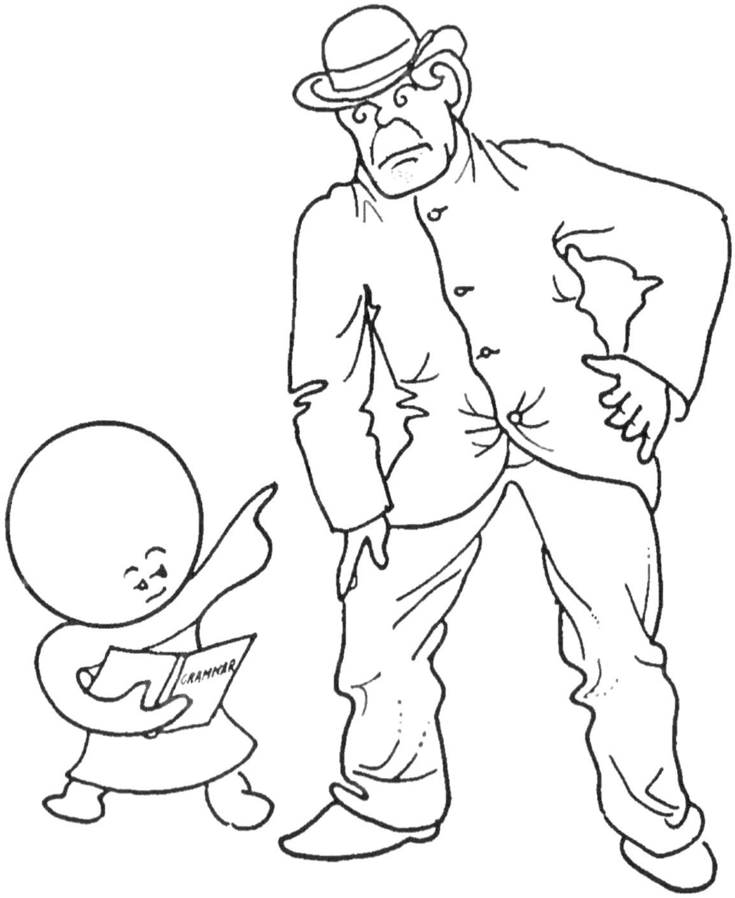
GRAMMAR

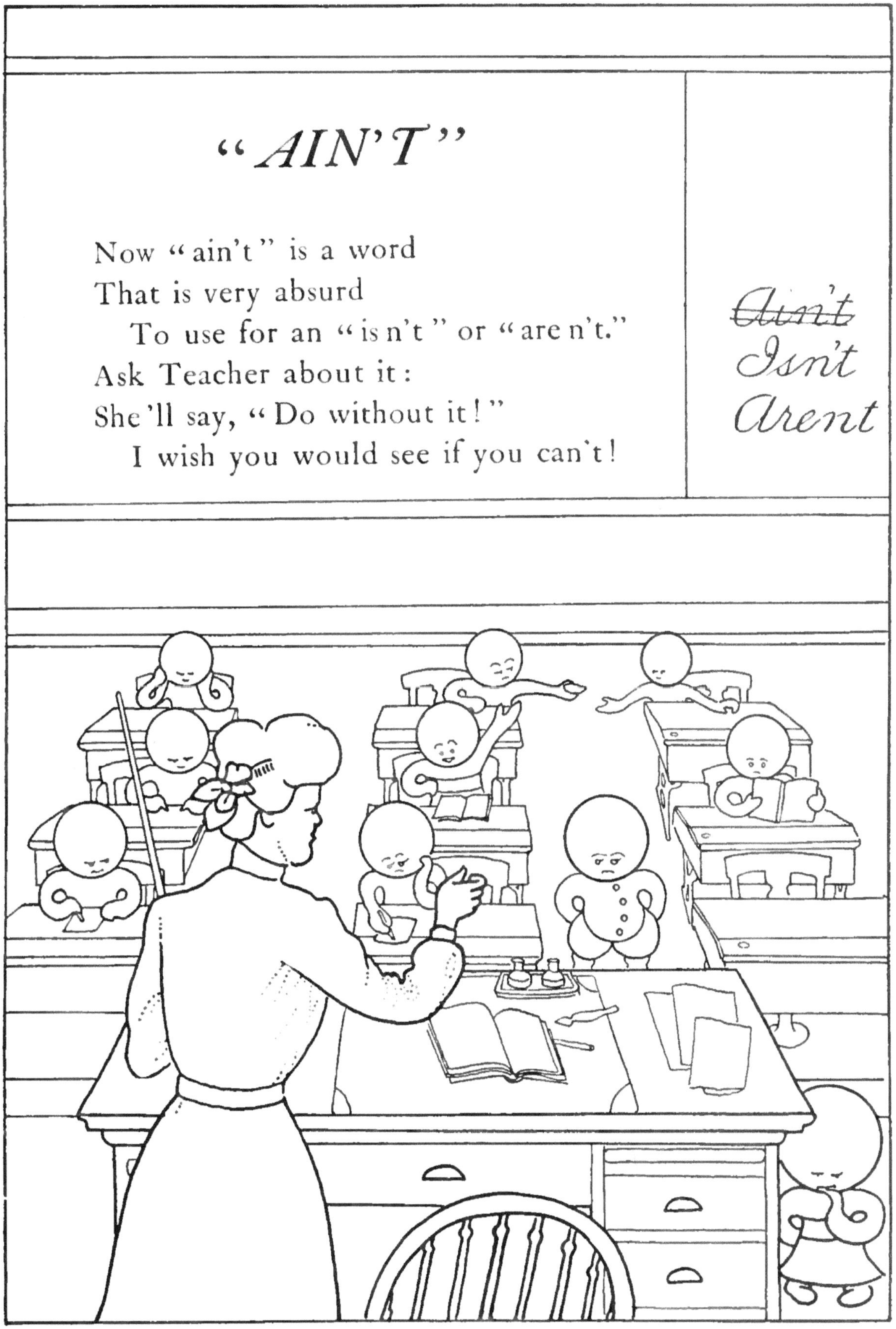
"AIN'T"
Now "ain't" is a word
That is very absurd
To use for an "is n't" or "are n't."
Ask Teacher about it:
She'll say, "Do without it!"
I wish you would see if you can't!
~~Ain't~~
Isn't
Arent

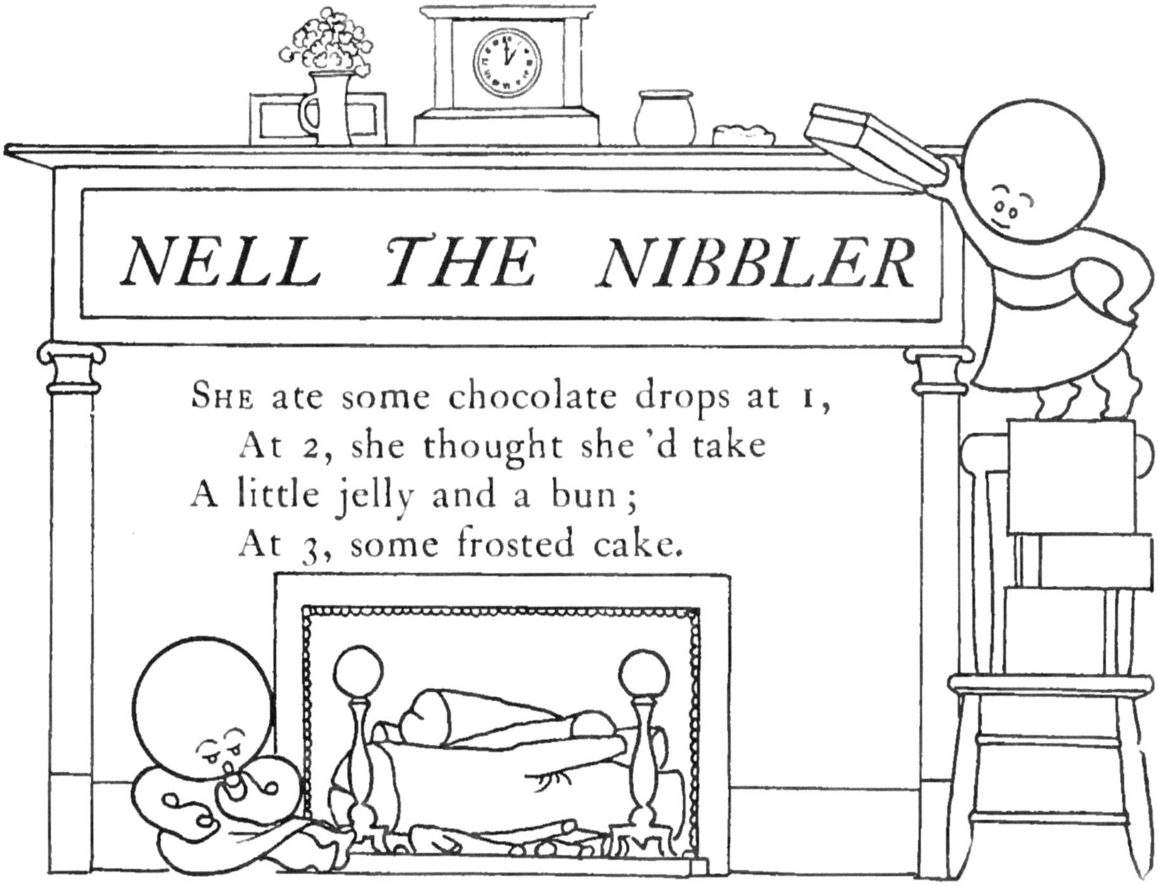

NELL THE NIBBLER

SHE ate some chocolate drops at 1,
At 2, she thought she 'd take
A little jelly and a bun;
At 3, some frosted cake.

At 4, she nibbled at a roll;
At 5, a doughnut spied,
And ate it (all except the hole),
And then some cookies tried.

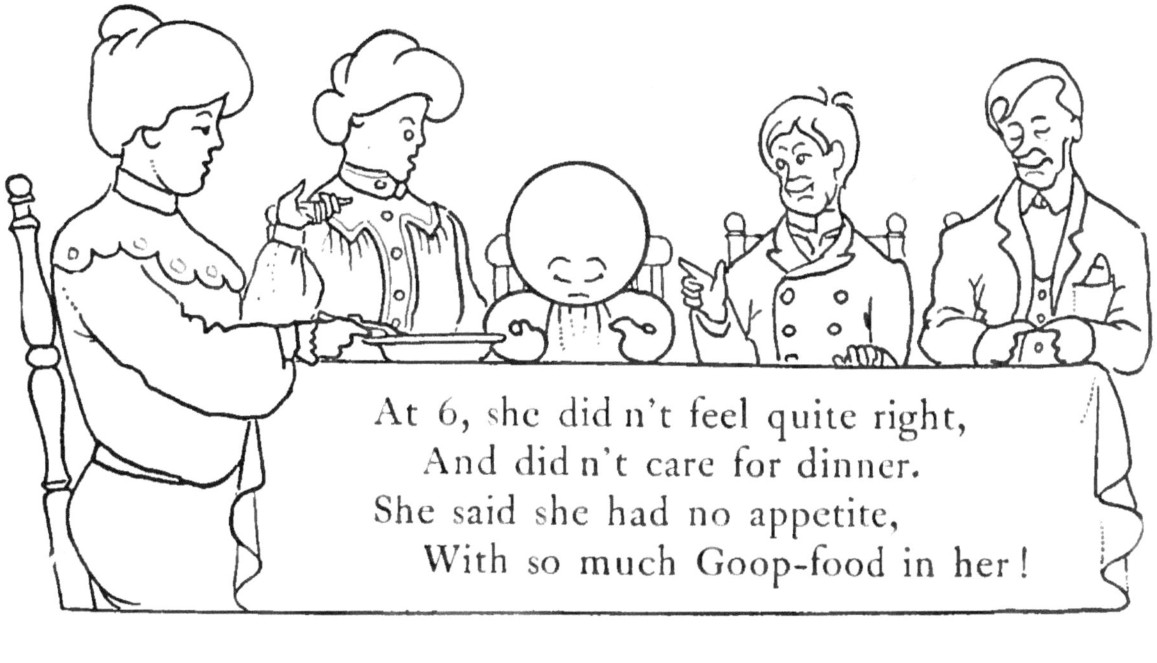

At 6, she did n't feel quite right,
And did n't care for dinner.
She said she had no appetite,
With so much Goop-food in her!

JUSTICE

WHENEVER brother's sent to bed,
　　Or punished, do not go
And peer at him and jeer at him,
　　And say, " I told you so ! "

Nor should you try to make him laugh
　　When he has been so bad ;
Let him confess his naughtiness
　　Before you both are glad !

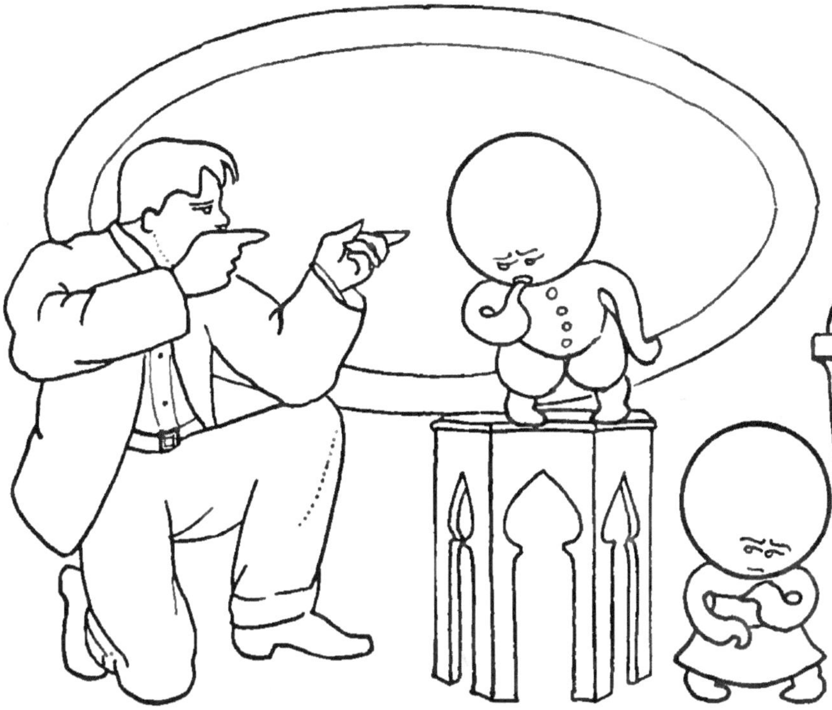

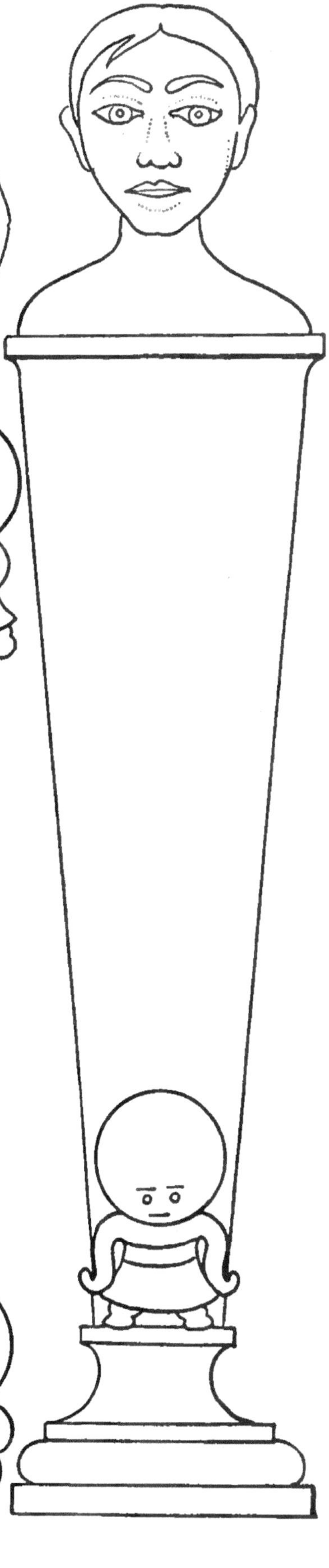

FRANKNESS

When you are talking, I expect
You 'd better hold your head erect!
Please look me squarely in the eye
Unless you 're telling me a lie.
For if you crouch and look askance,
Regarding me with sidelong glance,
I 'll think it is a Goop I see
Who is *afraid* to look at me!

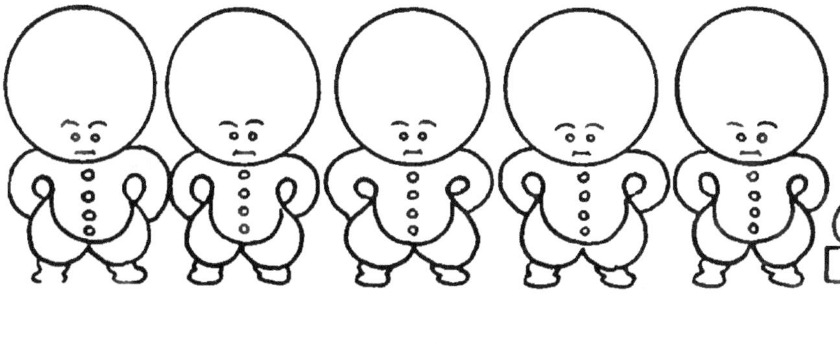

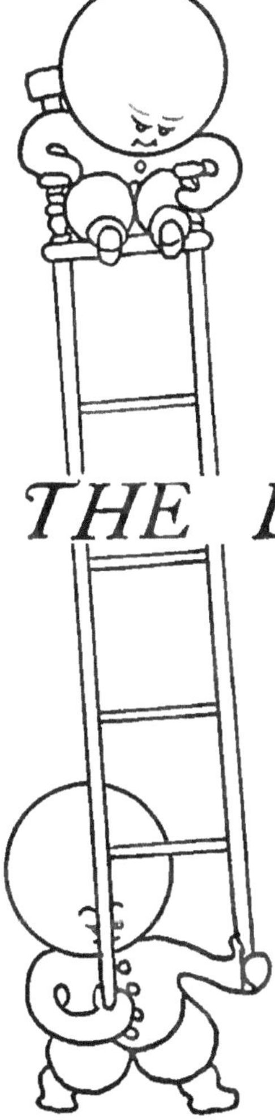

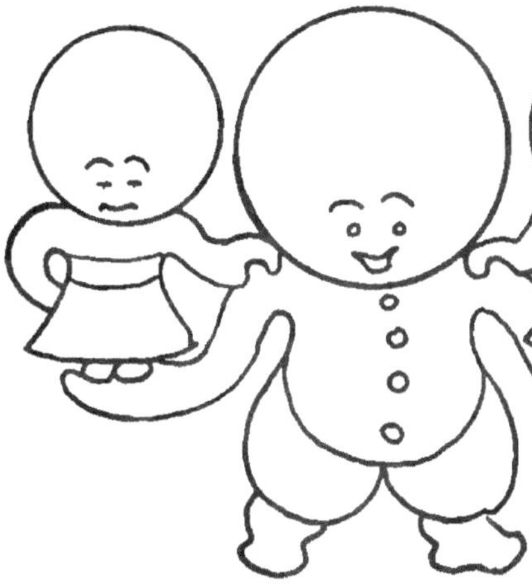

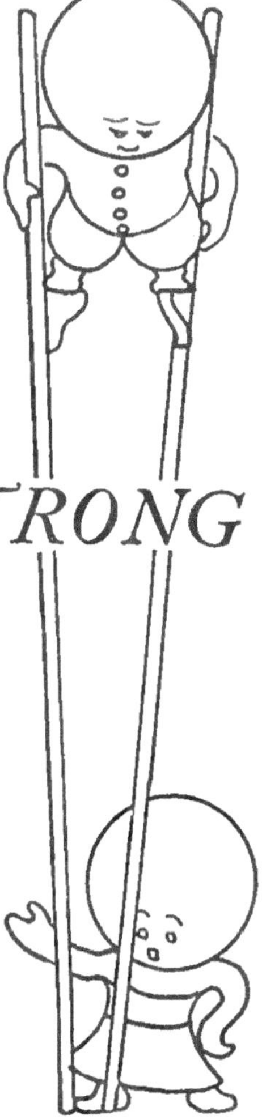

THE DUTY OF THE STRONG

You who are the oldest,
You who are the tallest,
Don't you think you ought to help
The youngest and the smallest?

You who are the strongest,
You who are the quickest,
Don't you think you ought to help
The weakest and the sickest?

Never mind the trouble,
Help them all you can;
Be a little woman!
Be a little man!

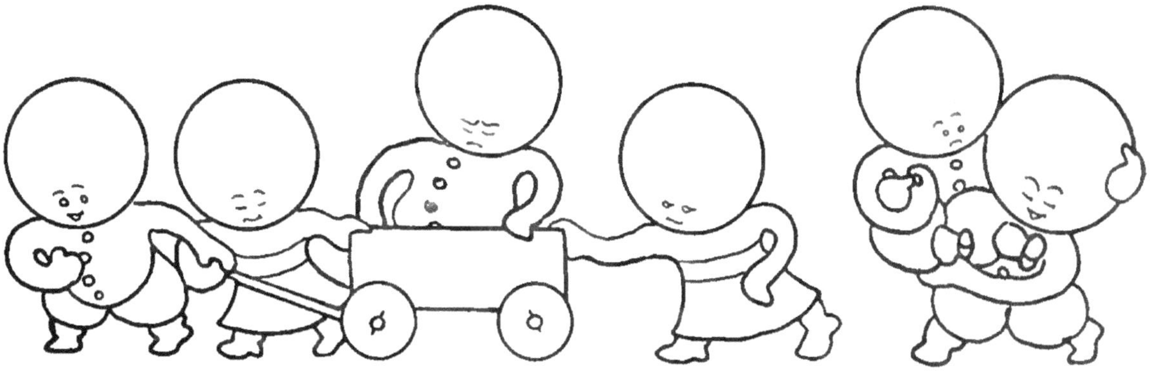

WALKING WITH PAPA

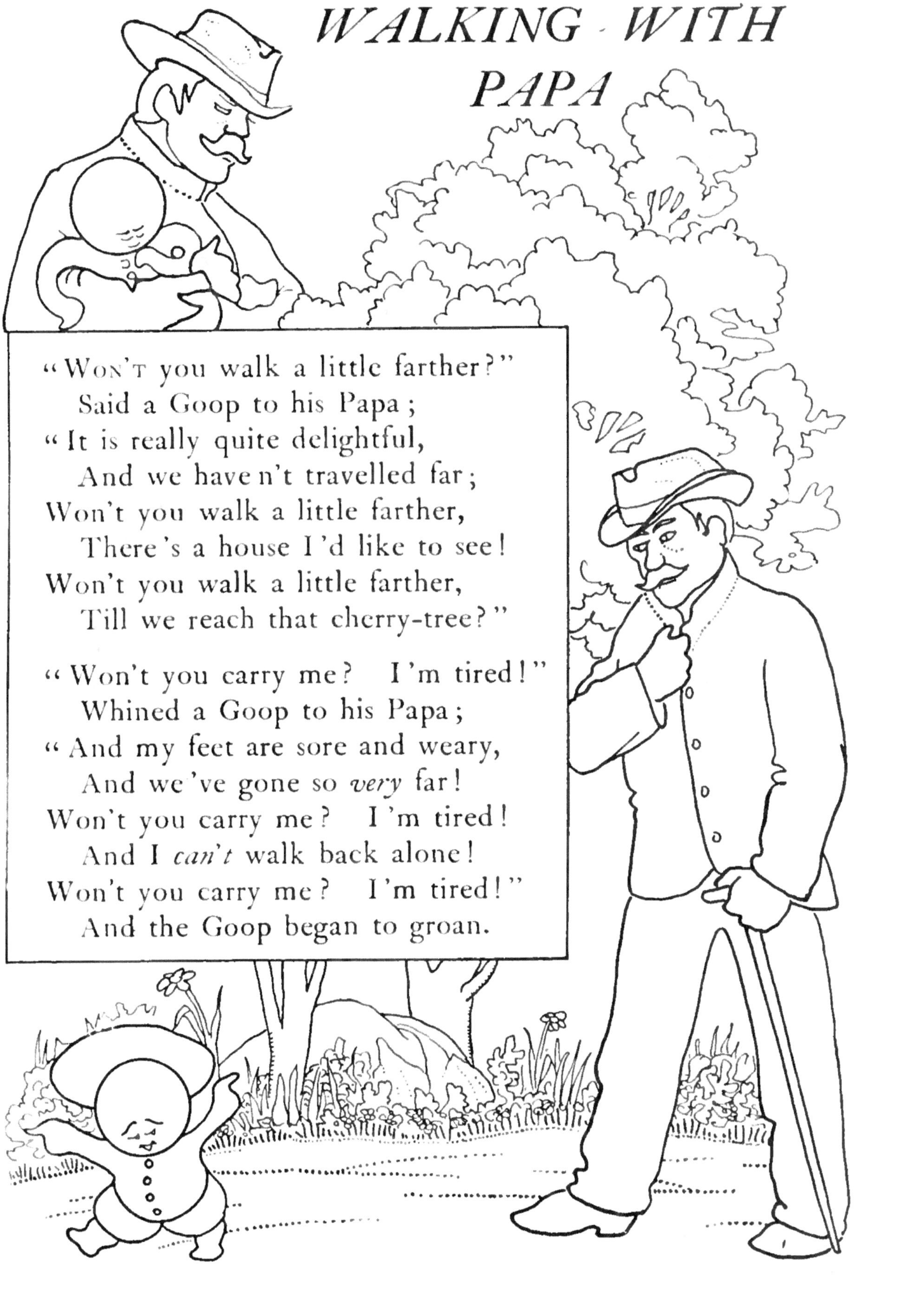

"WON'T you walk a little farther?"
Said a Goop to his Papa;
"It is really quite delightful,
And we have n't travelled far;
Won't you walk a little farther,
There's a house I'd like to see!
Won't you walk a little farther,
Till we reach that cherry-tree?"

"Won't you carry me? I'm tired!"
Whined a Goop to his Papa;
"And my feet are sore and weary,
And we've gone so *very* far!
Won't you carry me? I'm tired!
And I *can't* walk back alone!
Won't you carry me? I'm tired!"
And the Goop began to groan.

PIANO TORTURE

PIANOS are considered toys
By Goops, and naughty girls and boys;
   They pound upon the keys,
They lift the cover up, on top,
To see the little jiggers hop,
   And both the pedals squeeze!

But instruments so rich and fine
(Especially if they're not mine)
   I ought to treat with care;
So when my elder sister plays
She'll find it is in tune always,
   Nor injured anywhere!

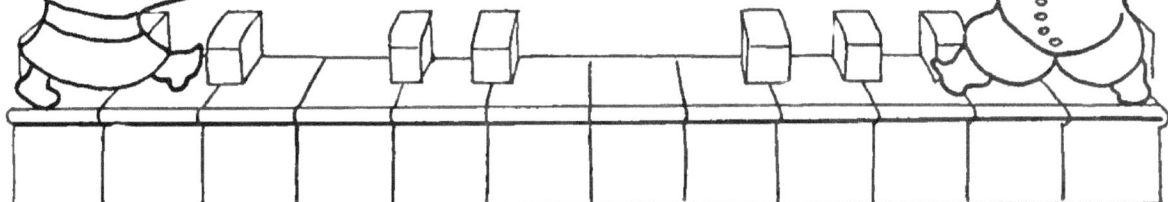

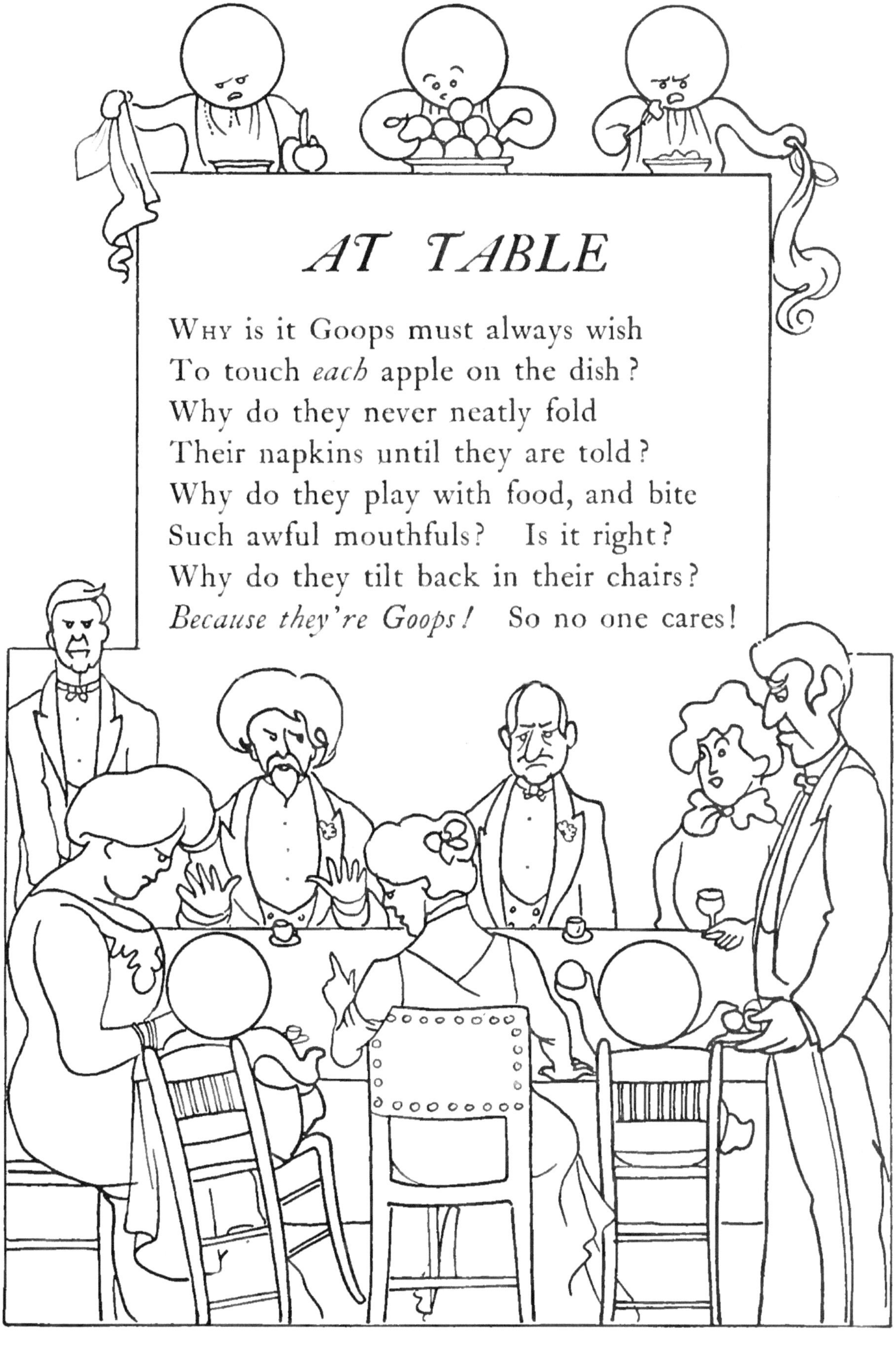

AT TABLE

WHY is it Goops must always wish
To touch *each* apple on the dish?
Why do they never neatly fold
Their napkins until they are told?
Why do they play with food, and bite
Such awful mouthfuls? Is it right?
Why do they tilt back in their chairs?
Because they're Goops! So no one cares!

HOW TO EAT SOUP

WHENEVER you are eating soup
Remember not to be a Goop!
And if you think to say this rhyme,
Perhaps 'twill help you every time:

Like little boats that put to sea,
I push my spoon AWAY from me;
I do not tilt my dish, nor scrape
The last few drops, like hungry ape!

Like little boats, that, almost filled,
Come back without their cargoes spilled,
My spoon sails gently to my lips,
Unloading from the SIDE, like ships.

NOTICE
DO NOT
WAKE UP
THIS SEED!

BABY'S APOLOGY

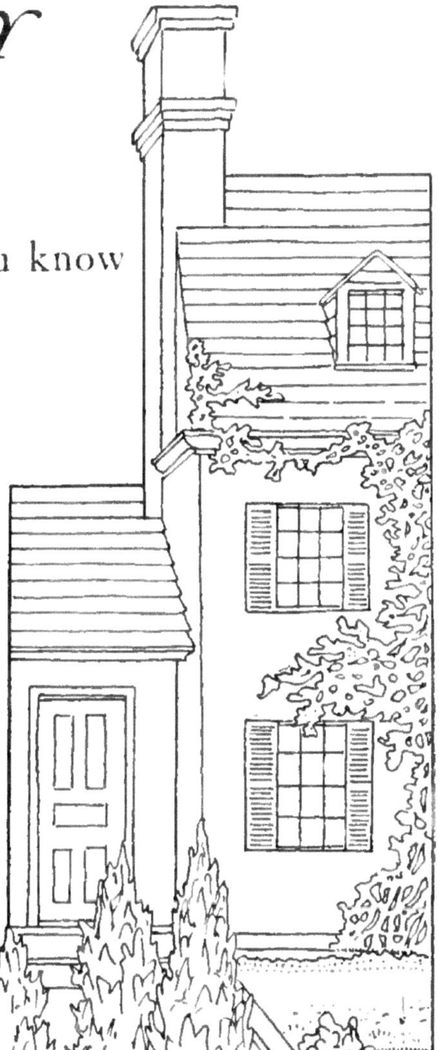

DEAR little seed, queer little seed,
  Tucked into bed in the garden,
Why don't you grow? Why, don't you know
  Baby is asking your pardon?

Out, little seed! Sprout, little seed!
  Baby did wrong without knowing!
Hoping for you, groping for you,
  To see if you *really* were growing.

Break, little seed! Wake, little seed!
  Baby will watch and not harm you.
Everything 's bright, everything 's right,
  Nothing is here to alarm you.

Dress, little seed! Yes, little seed,
  Fold your green leaflets around you;
There, little seed! Fair little seed,
  Baby's *so* glad he has found you!

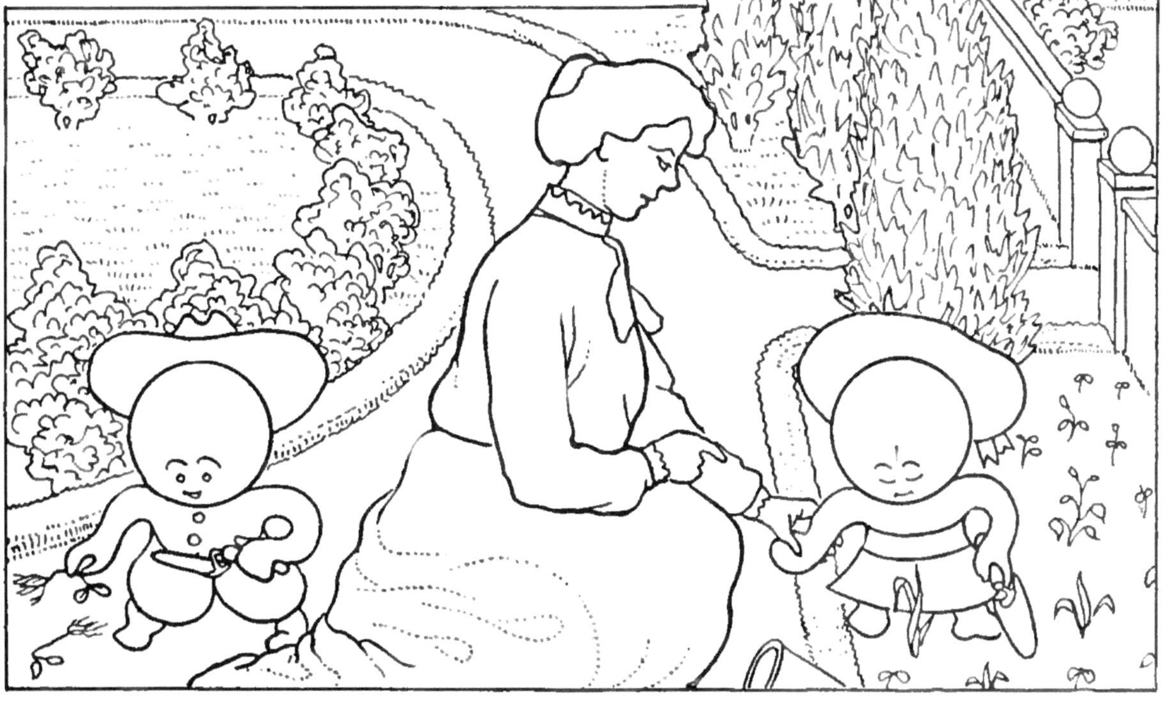

IN THE STREET

Peelings on the sidewalk,
  Apple-cores and all,
Kick them in the gutter;
  Save some one a fall!
Barrel hoops, glass, and cans,
  And wires in the street,
Kick them in the gutter;
  You'll save some horse's feet!

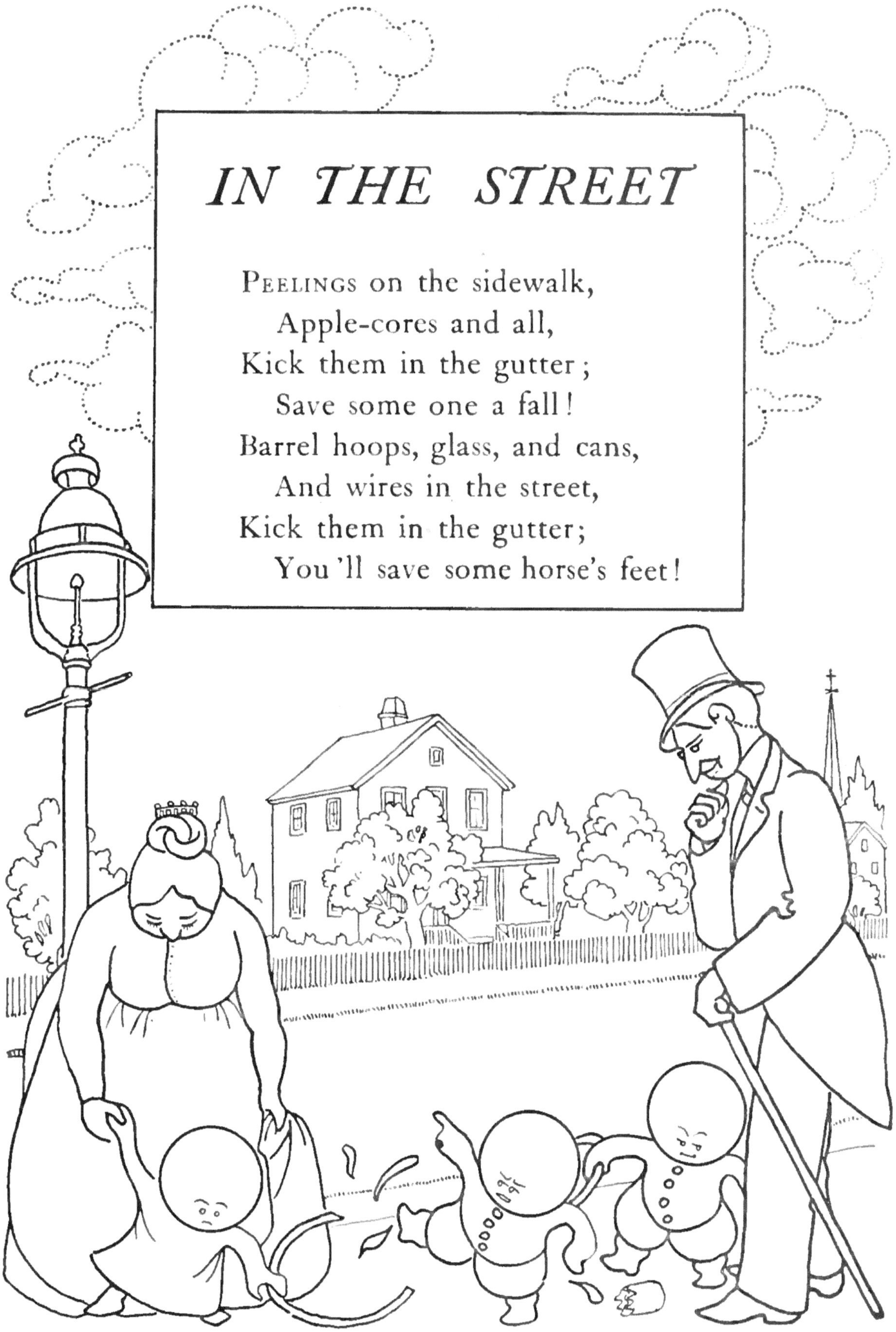

SICK FURNITURE

SITTING on the table,
Standing on the chairs,
That's the way the legs are broken
and the cushion tears!
How'd you like to pay the bill for varnish and repairs?

BORROWED PLUMES

Don't try on the wraps,
The bonnets and caps
    Of company coming to call!
Admire, if you please,
But garments like these
    Should always feel safe in the hall!

THE GOOP PICNIC

THEY came to the best sort of place for a rest,
  On the grass, with the trees overhead,
They sat down in a bunch and they opened their
    lunch,
  And they had a be-autiful spread!

And when they were done, and they'd had all their
    fun,
  They proved they were Goops, or were blind;
For they picked up their wraps and they left all their
    scraps
  For the *next* picnic party to find!

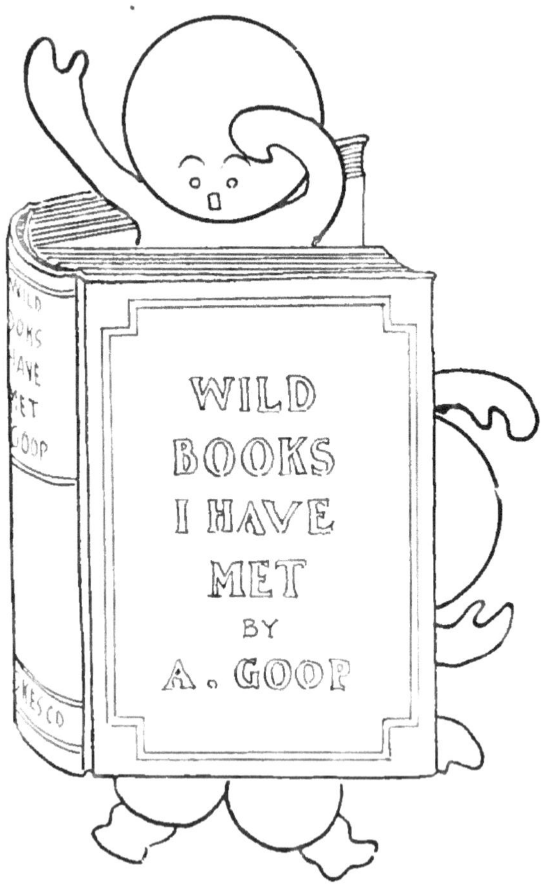
WILD
BOOKS
I HAVE
MET
BY
A. GOOP

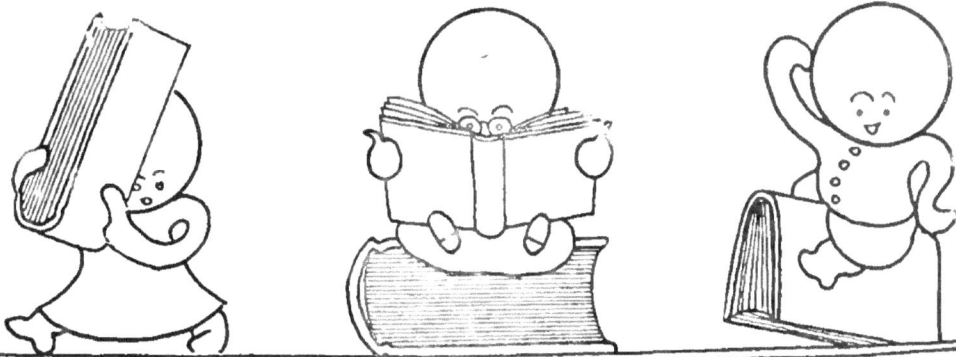

BOOK-MANNERS

IF you scribble on your books,
How disgustable it looks!
Here a word, and there a scrawl,
Silly pictures over all!
Take a paper, or a slate,
If you want to decorate!

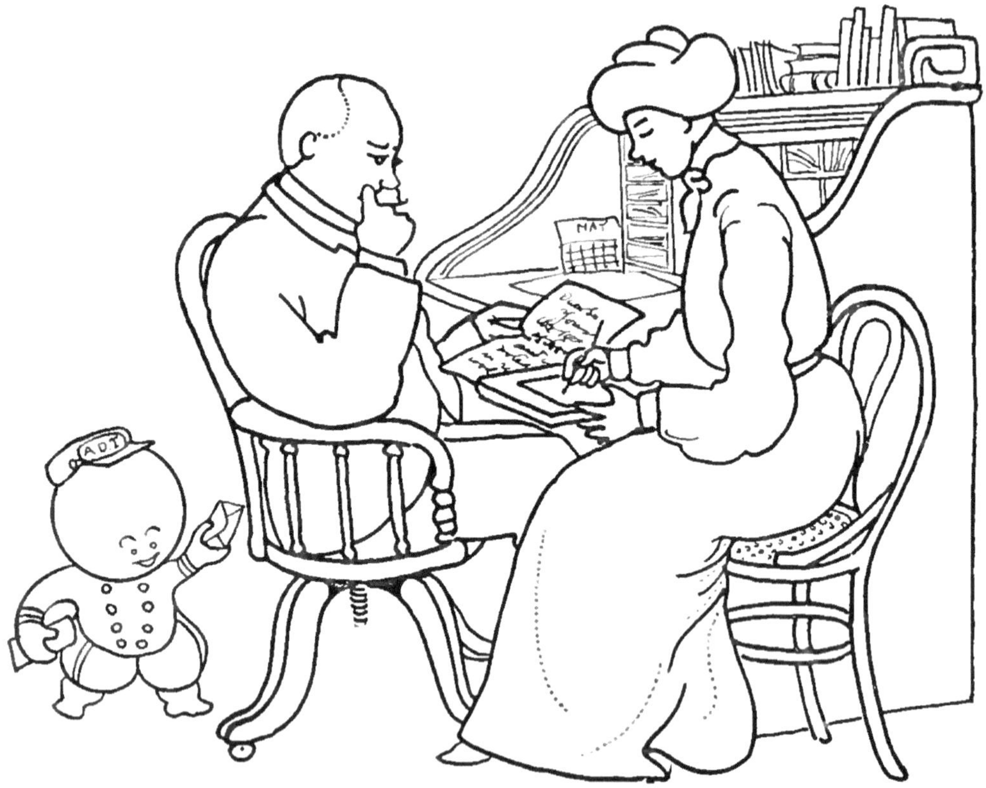
MAY
ADT

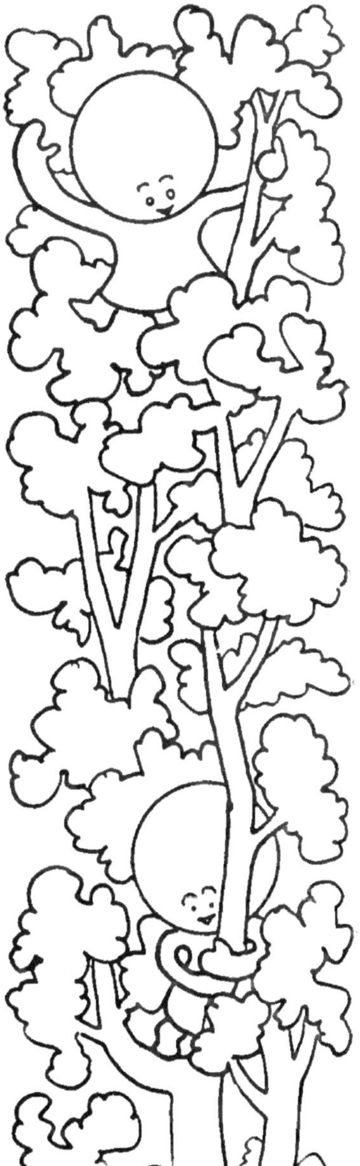

POOR MOTHER!

OH! Is n't it shocking!
Just look at your stocking!
  Just look at your brand new boots!
Your waist is all torn
And your trousers are worn —
  Just *look* at the holes in your suits!

Your father is working
All day, without shirking,
  To pay for the clothes that you wear;
Your mother is mending
All day, and attending
  To you, with the kindest of care.

And so, while you 're playing,
Think of father, who 's paying,
  And mother, who 's working so hard;
While you kneel on your knees,
Or climb up the trees,
  Or make your mud pies in the yard!

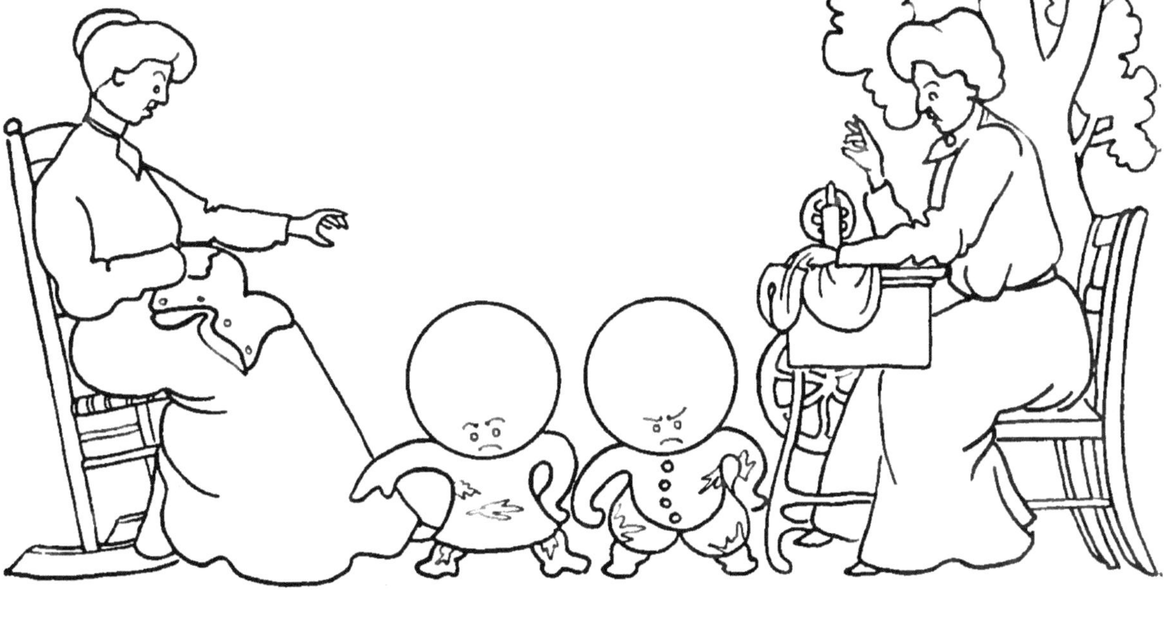

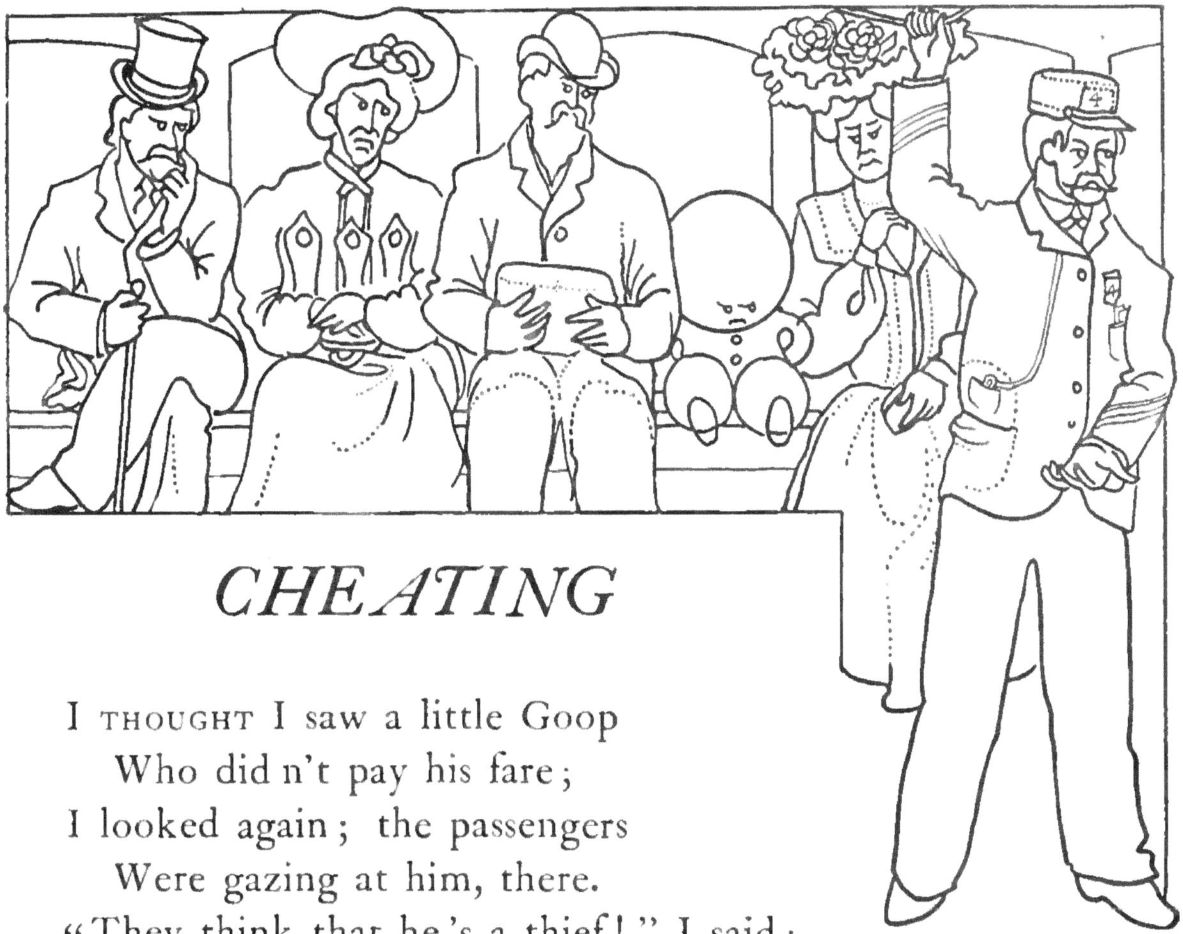

CHEATING

I THOUGHT I saw a little Goop
  Who did n't pay his fare;
I looked again; the passengers
  Were gazing at him, there.
"They think that he's a thief!" I said;
  "I wonder does he care?"

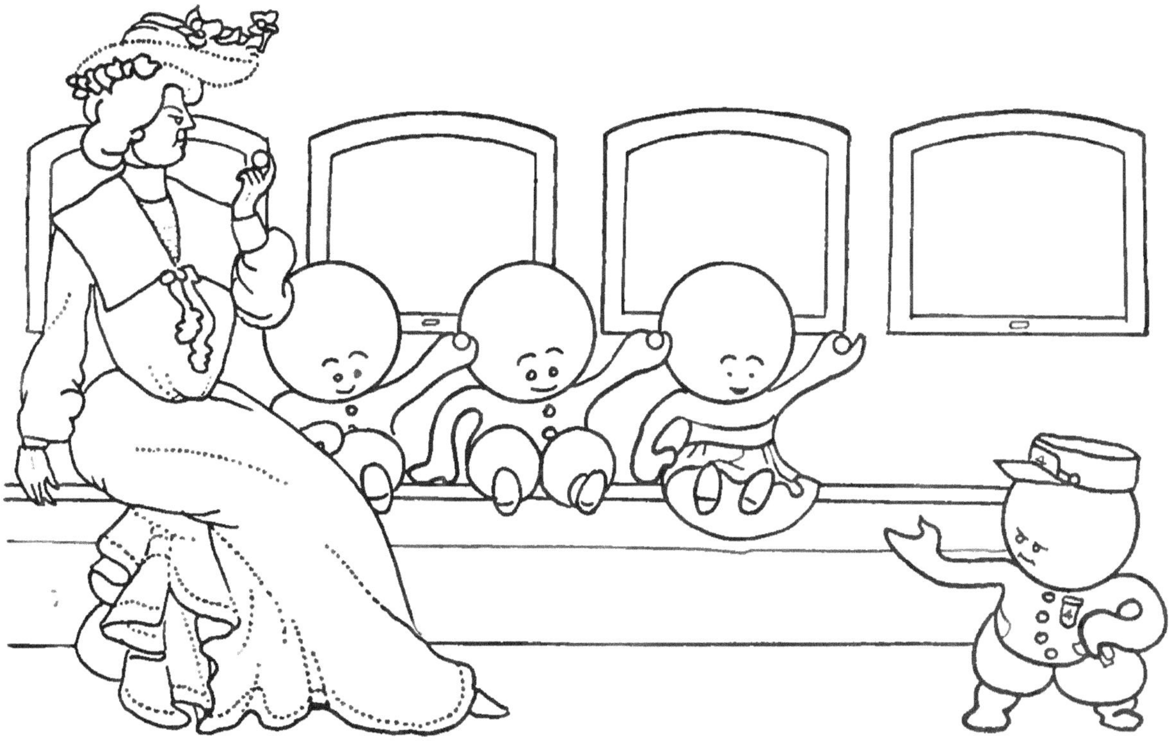

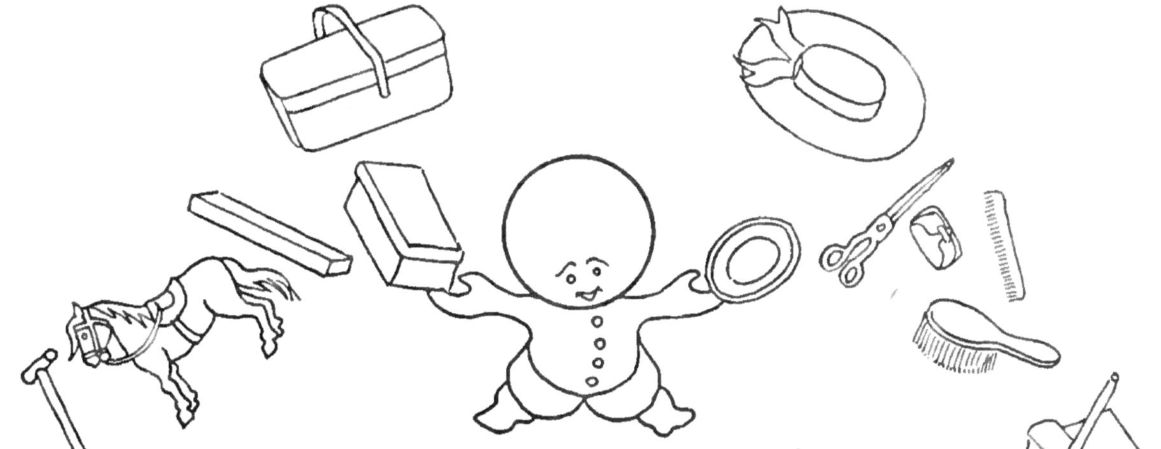

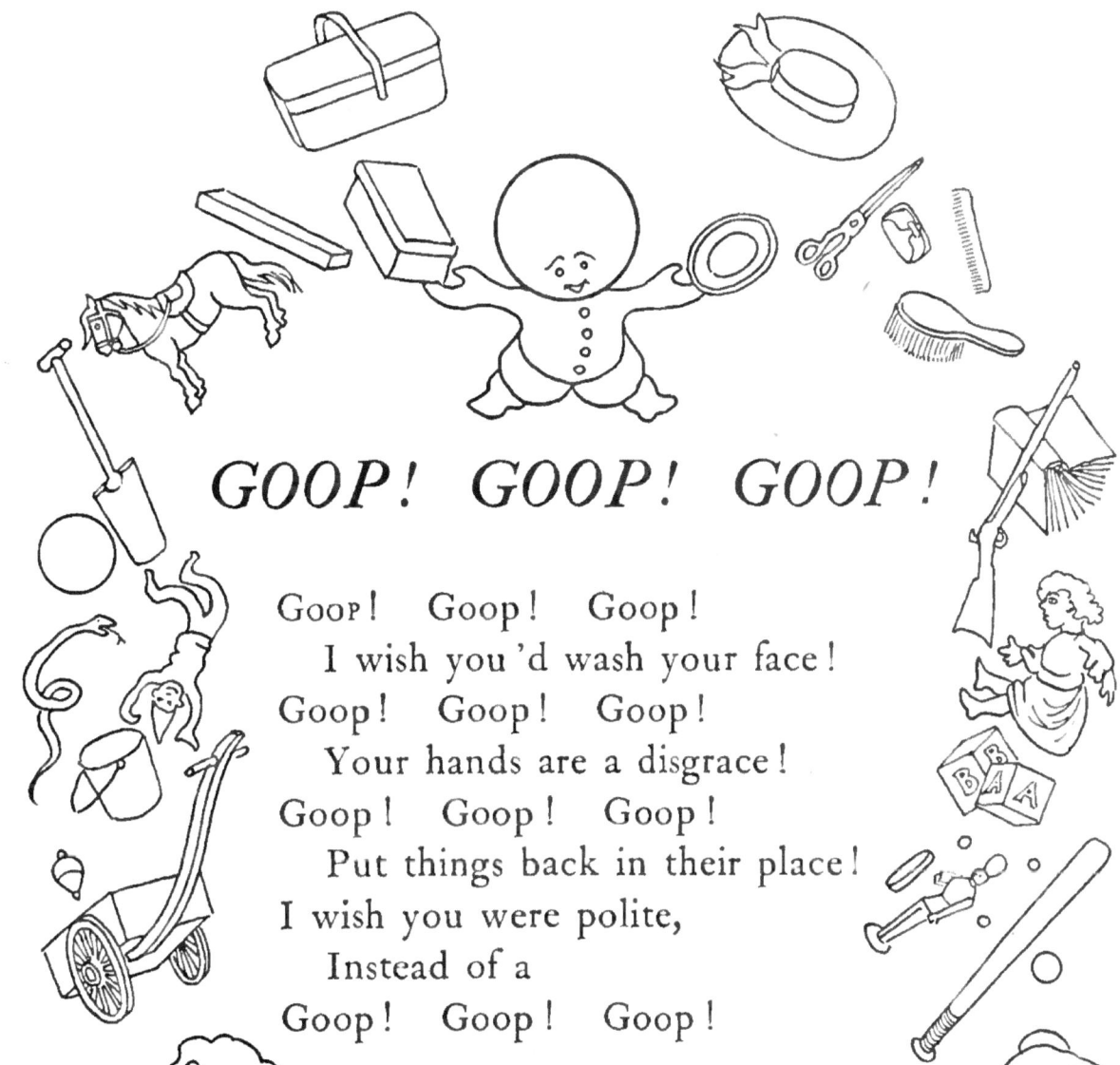

GOOP! GOOP! GOOP!

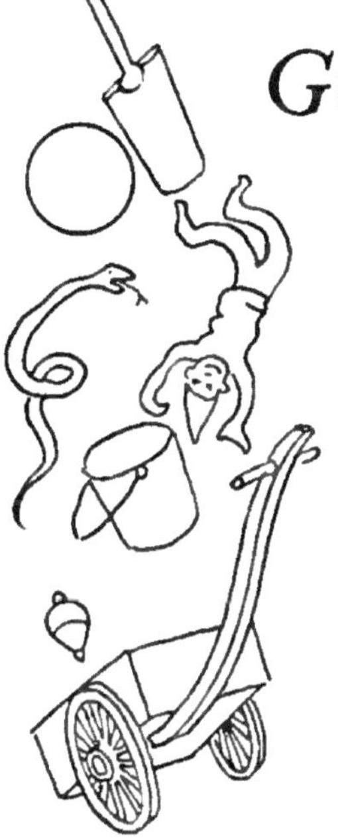

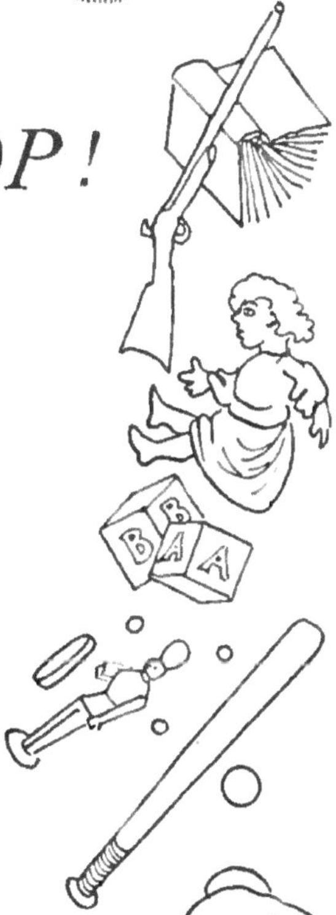

Goop! Goop! Goop!
  I wish you'd wash your face!
Goop! Goop! Goop!
  Your hands are a disgrace!
Goop! Goop! Goop!
  Put things back in their place!
I wish you were polite,
  Instead of a
Goop! Goop! Goop!

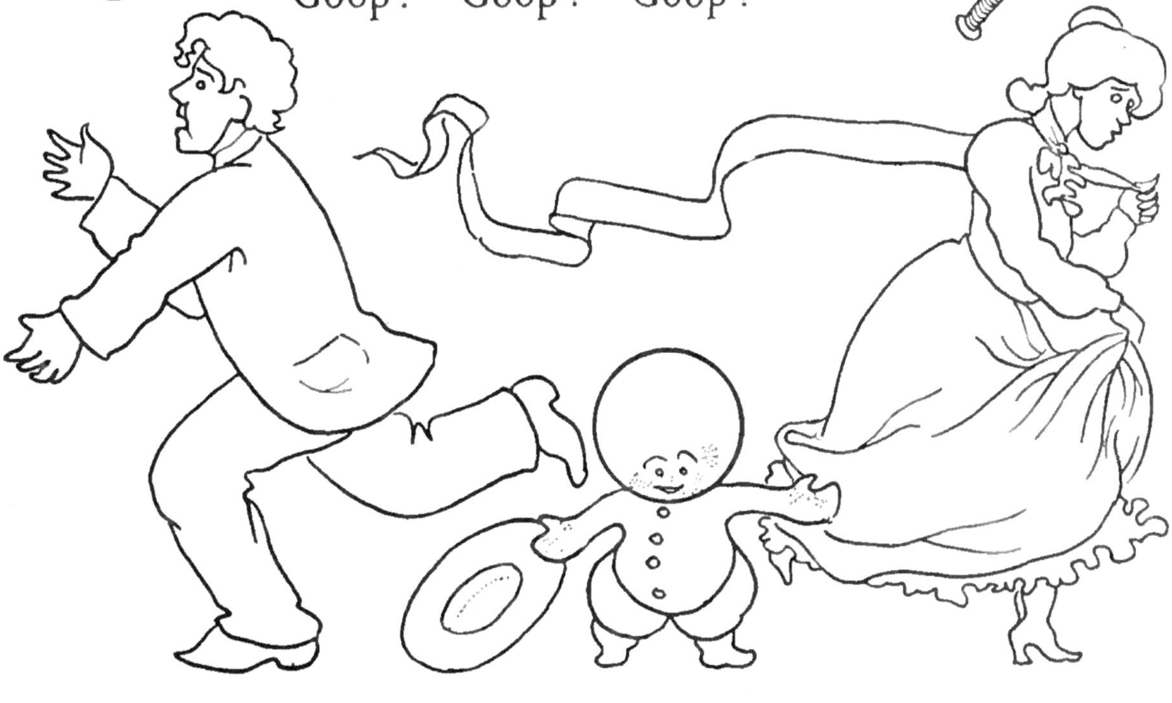

VISITING

WHEN a Goop goes out to visit,
'Tisn't very pleasant, is it,
> To hear him ask his friends for
> things to eat?
And to hear the little sinner
Say he wants to stay to dinner
> Is a piece of impoliteness hard to
> beat!
" *Mother said that I could stay*
" *If you asked me!* " is the way
> That a Goop will make them ask
> him to remain.
It is better to be slighted
Than to stay when not invited,
> For they *never* ask a Goop to
> come again!

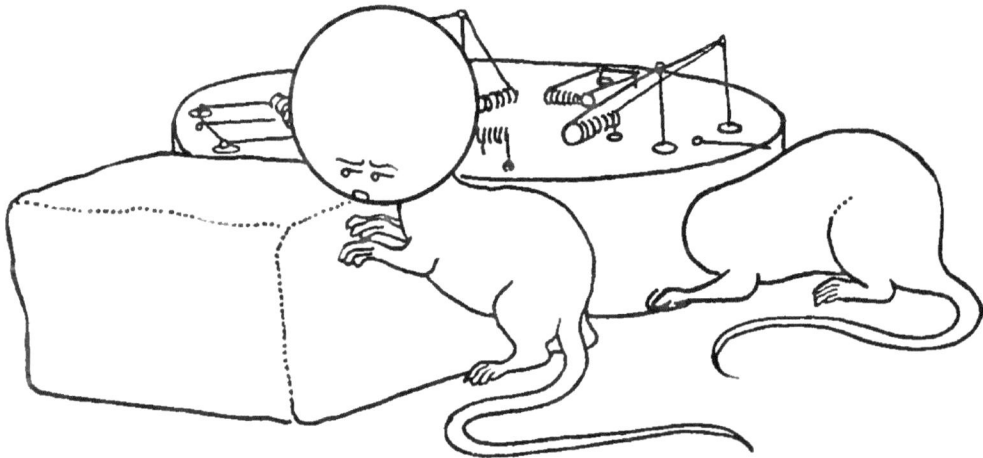

PICKING and STEALING

WHEN you are fetching bread, I trust
You never nibble at the crust.

When in the kitchen, do you linger
And pinch the cookies with your finger?

Or do you peck the frosted cake?
Don't do it, please, for Mother's sake!

LOYALTY

MOTHER's found your mischief out!
  What are you going to do?
Cry and sulk, or kick and shout?
Tell your mother all about
  Brother's mischief, too?

Or,
Take your punishment, and say,
  "I 'll be better, now!"
Never mind the horrid way
Brother treated you, at play;
  Don't tell it, anyhow!

It is the Goops,

  who have no shame,

Who say,

"'Twas some one else to blame!"

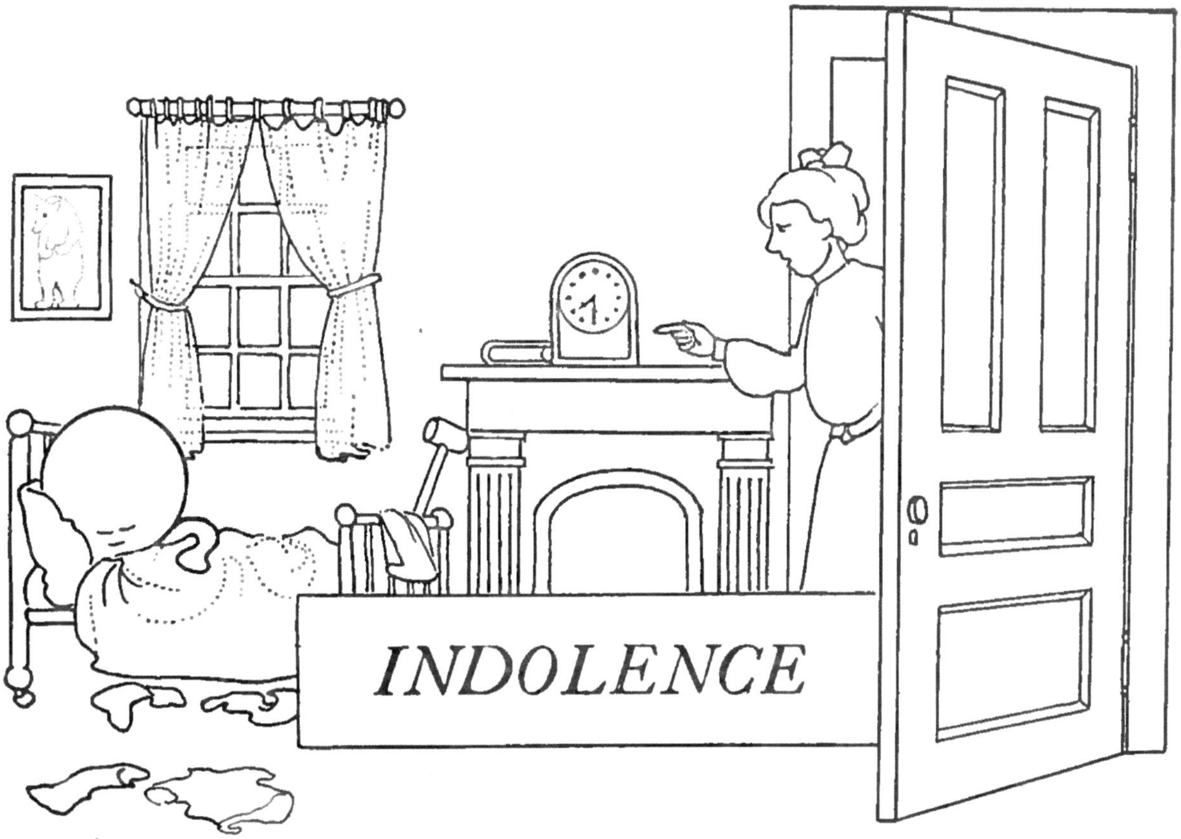
INDOLENCE

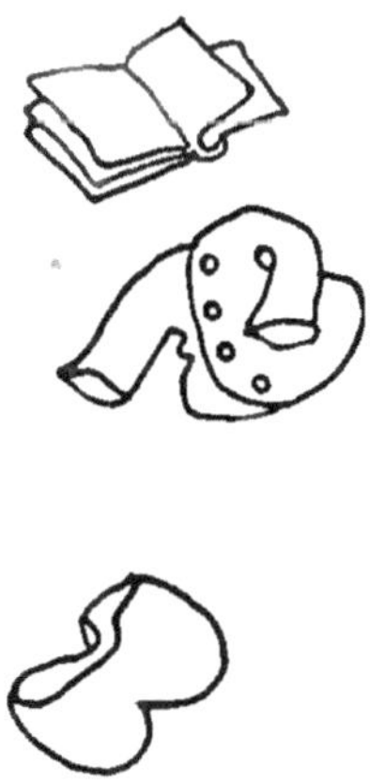

There was a Goop who lay in bed
Till half-past eight, the sleepy-head!
He could n't find his stockings, for
He 'd thrown them somewhere on the floor!
He could n't find his reading-book;
He had forgotten where to look!
His breakfast grew so very cold,
This lazy Goop began to scold;
And then he blamed his mother, kind!
"*You made me late to school!*"
he whined.

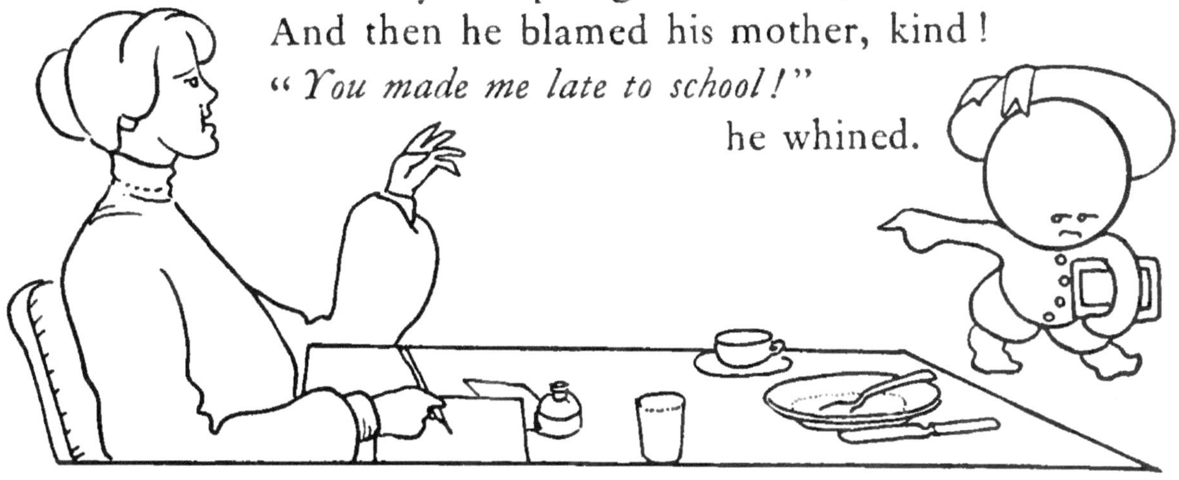

THE LAW OF HOSPITALITY

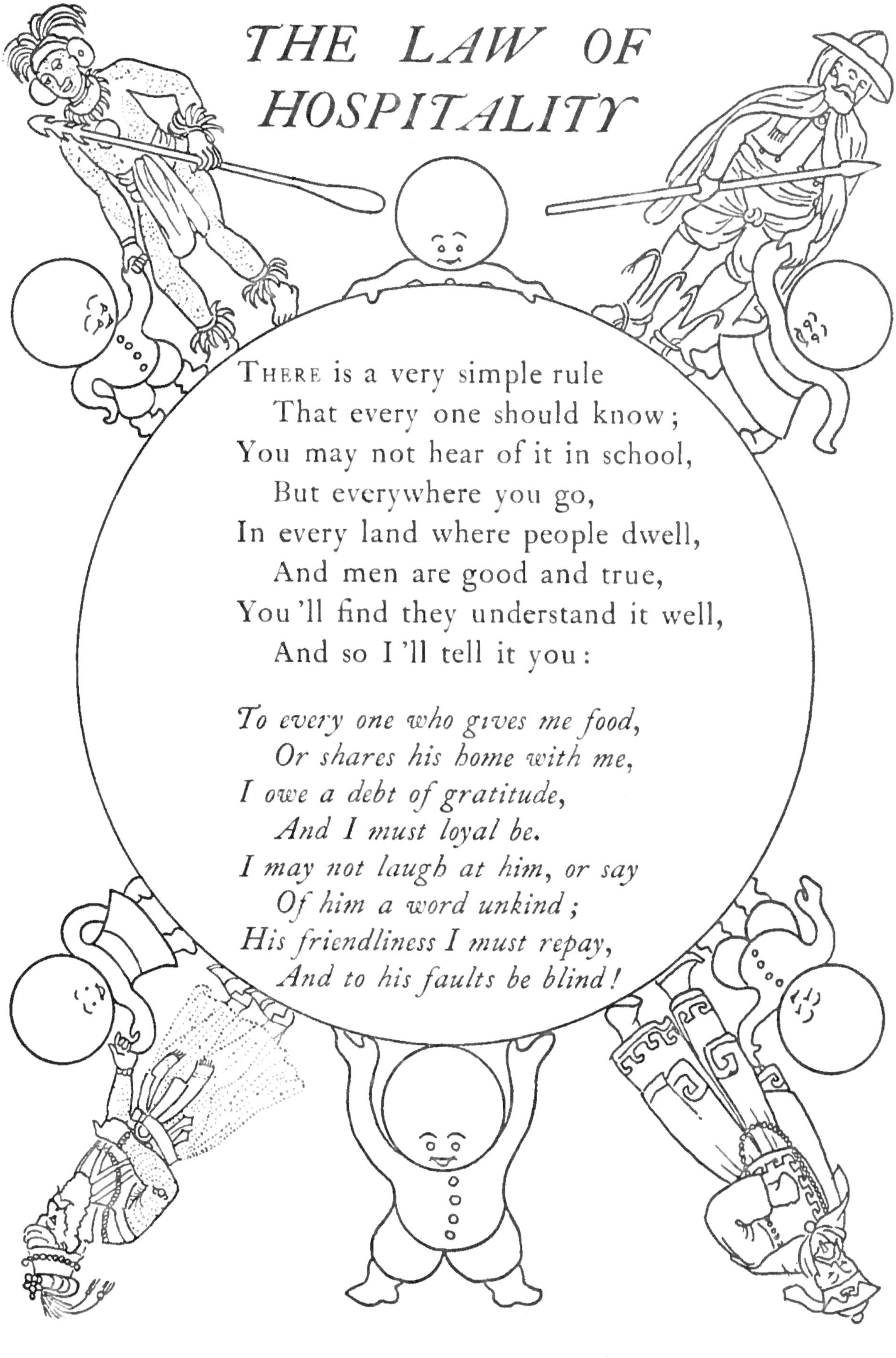

THERE is a very simple rule
  That every one should know;
You may not hear of it in school,
  But everywhere you go,
In every land where people dwell,
  And men are good and true,
You'll find they understand it well,
  And so I'll tell it you:

To every one who gives me food,
  Or shares his home with me,
I owe a debt of gratitude,
  And I must loyal be.
I may not laugh at him, or say
  Of him a word unkind;
His friendliness I must repay,
  And to his faults be blind!

THE · FLOWER HOSPITAL

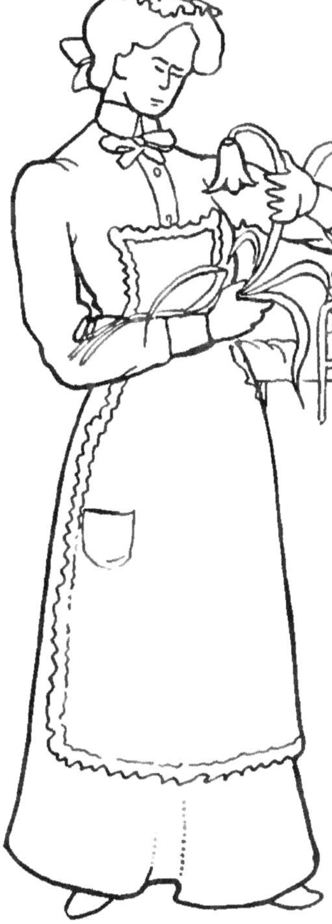

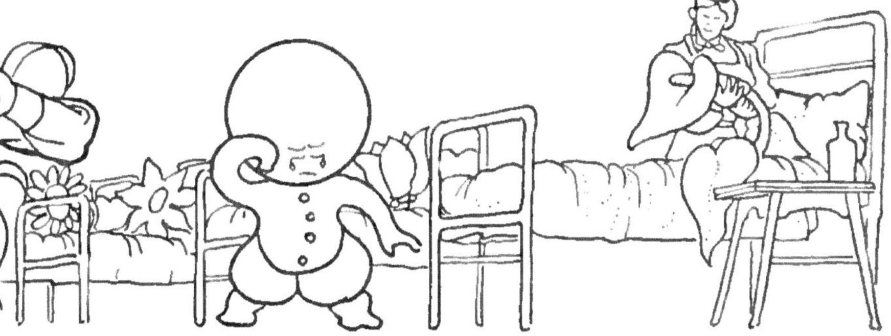

I DREAMED I found a sunlit room
Filled with a delicate perfume,
Where, moaning their sweet lives away,
A thousand lovely flowers lay.
They drooped, so pale, and wan, and weak,
With hardly strength enough to speak,
With stems so crushed and leaves so torn
It was too dreadful to be borne!
And one white lily raised her head
From off her snowy flower bed,
And sighed, "*Please tell the children, oh!*
They should not treat the flowers so!
They plucked us when we were so gay,
And then they threw us all away
To wither in the sun all day!
We all must fade, but we'll forgive
If they'll let other flowers live!"

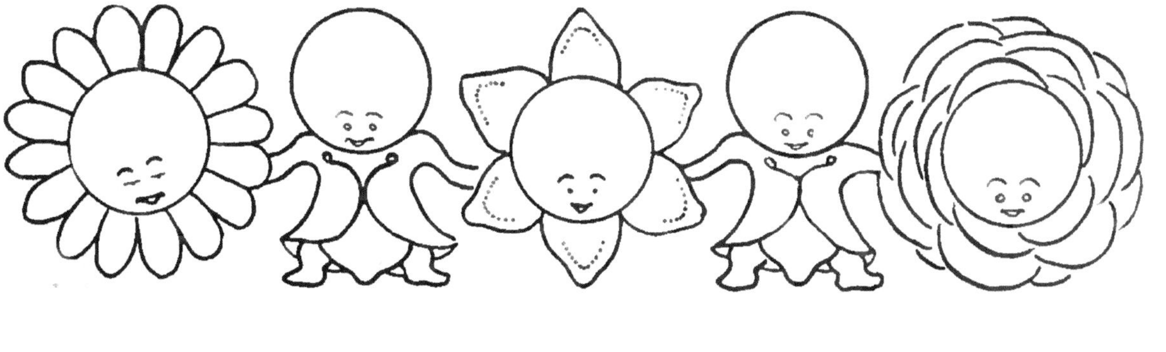

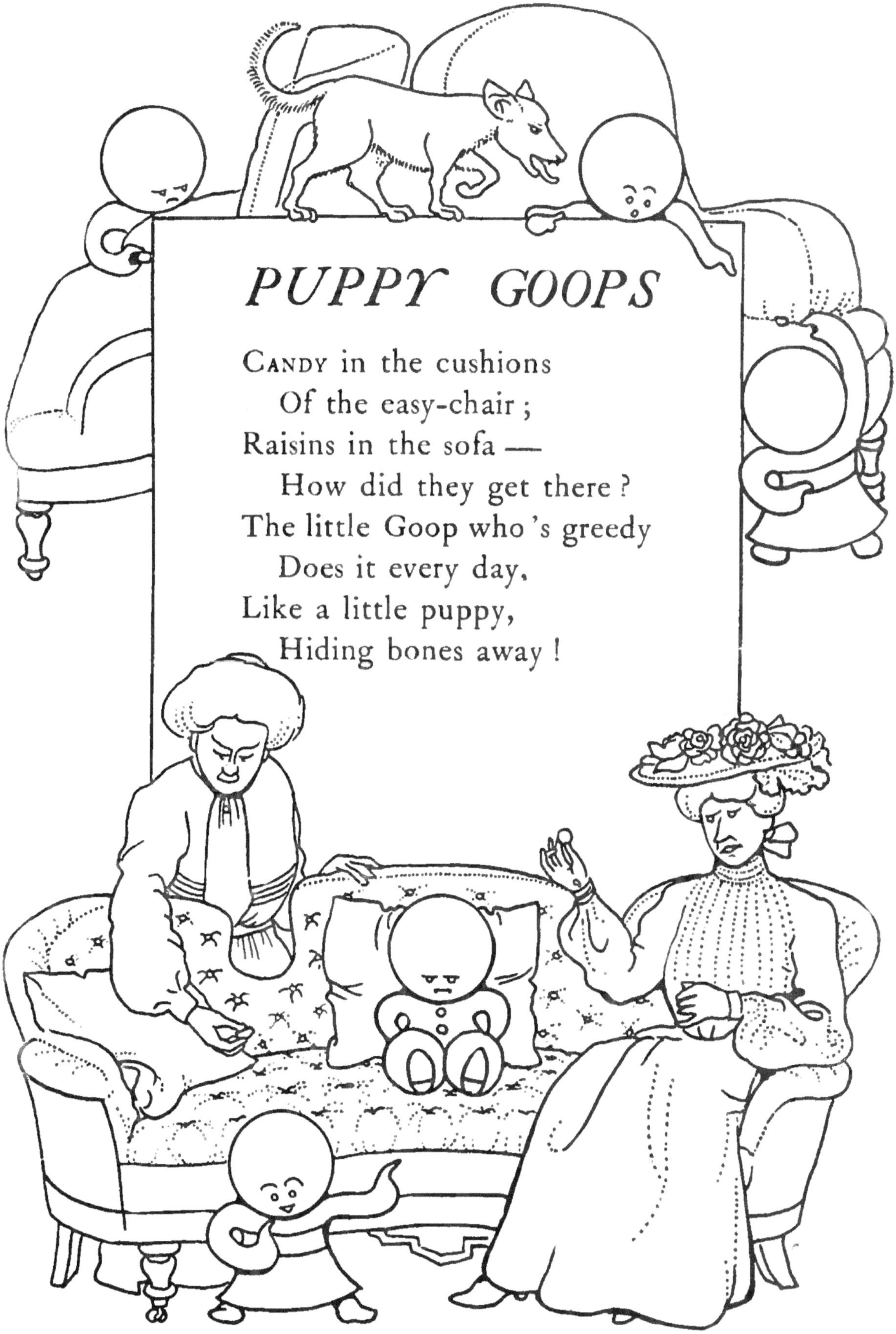

PUPPY GOOPS

Candy in the cushions
  Of the easy-chair;
Raisins in the sofa —
  How did they get there?
The little Goop who's greedy
  Does it every day,
Like a little puppy,
  Hiding bones away!

EXAGGERATION

Don't try to tell a story
    To beat the one you've heard;
For if you try, you're apt to lie,
    And *that* would be absurd!

Don't try to be more funny
    Than any one in school;
For if you're not, they'll laugh a lot,
    And think you are a fool!

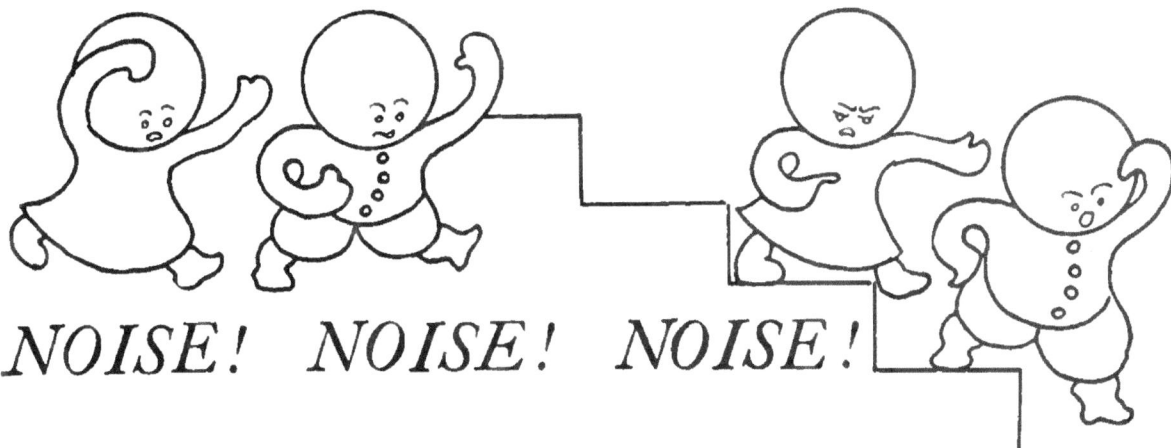

NOISE! NOISE! NOISE!

Do you slam the door?
  Do you drag your feet?
Making noise enough for four
Hundred thousand Goops, or more,
  Tearing up the street?

Clattering down the stairs,
  Storming through the hall,
Pounding floors, upsetting chairs,
Do you think your father cares
  For your noise, at all?

STEALING RIDES

I THOUGHT I saw a little Goop
  Who hung behind a cart;
I looked again.   He'd fallen off!
  It gave me *such* a start!
"If he were killed, some day," I said,
  "'T would break his mother's heart!"

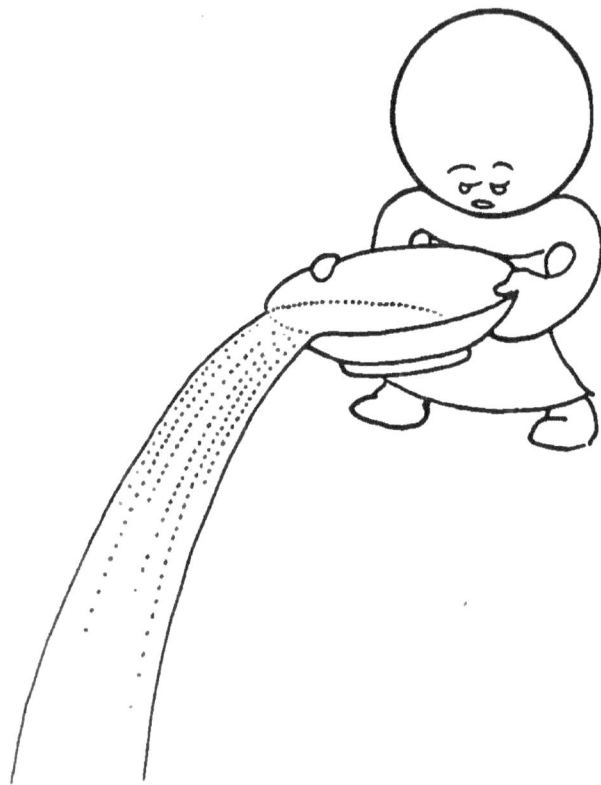

UNTIDY GOOPS

I THINK you are a Goop, because
You never shut your bureau drawers,
   You do not close the door!
You leave your water in the bowl,
You put your peelings in the coal!
   I've told you *that* before!

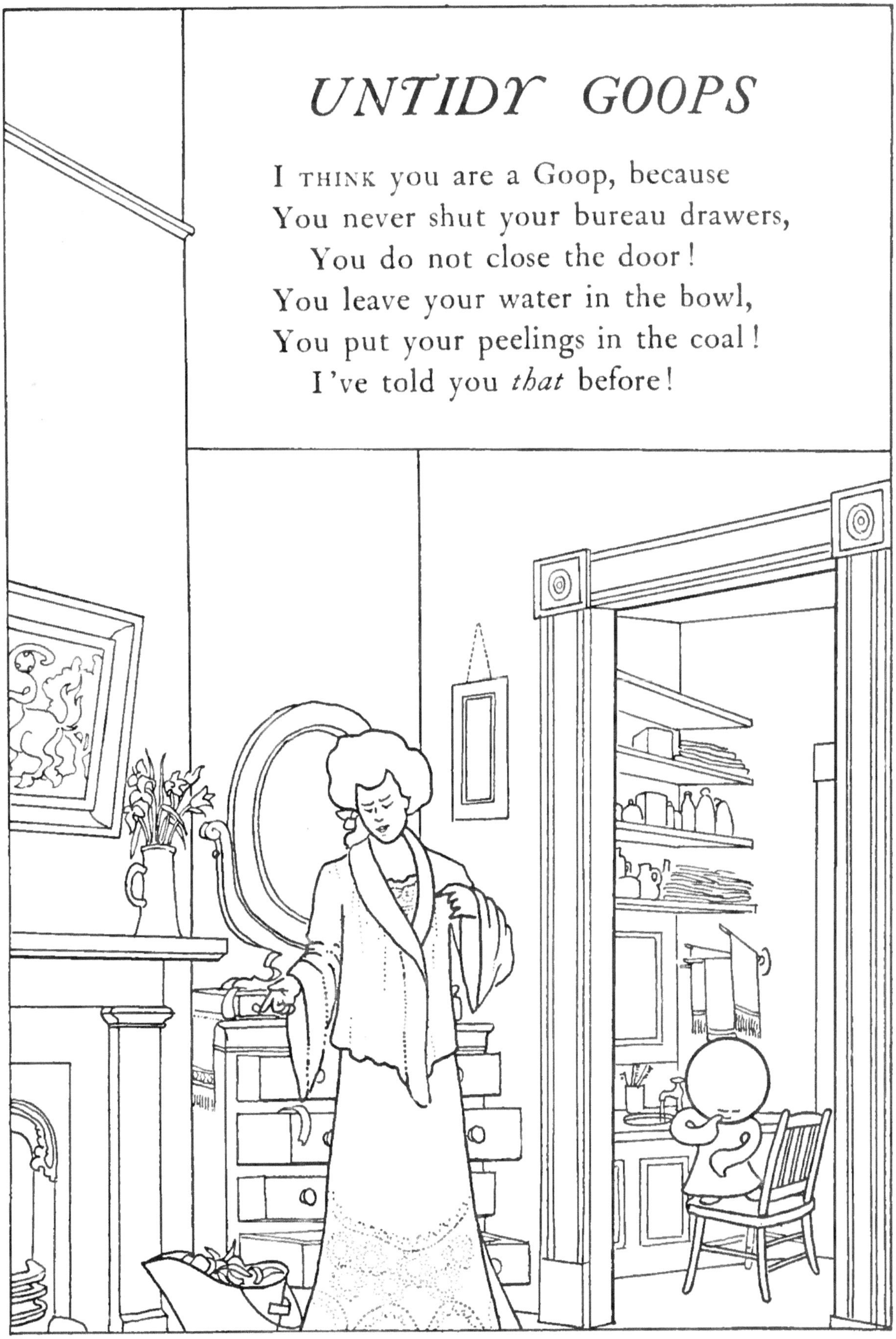

A GOOP PARTY

" PLEASE come to my party!" said Jenny to Prue;
" I 'm going to have Willy, and Nelly, and you;
I 'm going to have candy and cake and ice-cream,
We 'll play *Hunt-the-Slipper*, we 'll laugh and we 'll scream.
We 'll dress up in caps, we 'll have stories and tricks,
And you won't have to go till a quarter past six!"
But alas!   When she mentioned her party, at tea,
Her mother said, "No!   It can't possibly be!"
So Jane had to go and explain to her friends,
And that is how many a Goop party ends!
Just speak to your mother *before* you invite,
And then it 's more likely to happen all right!

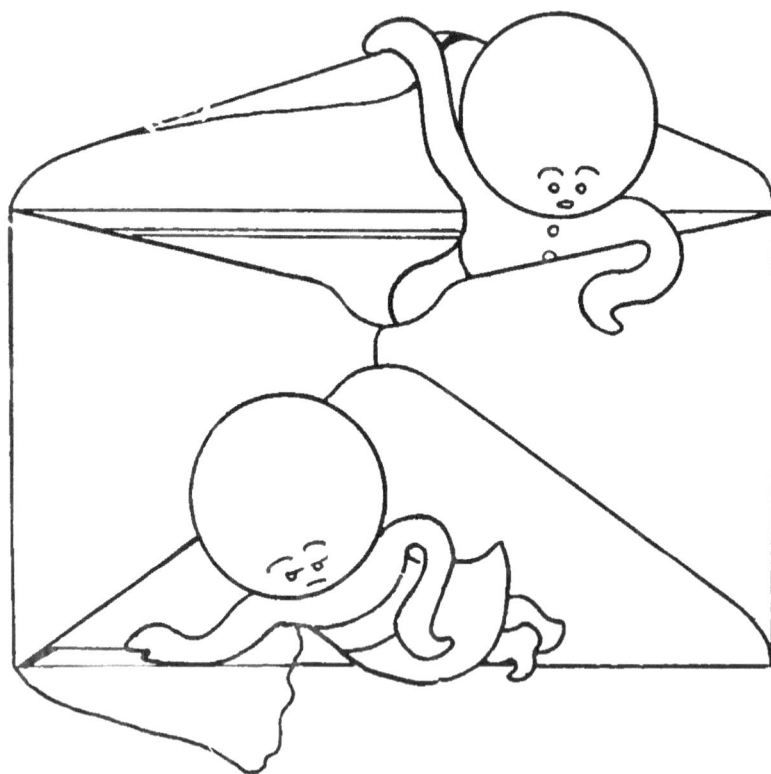

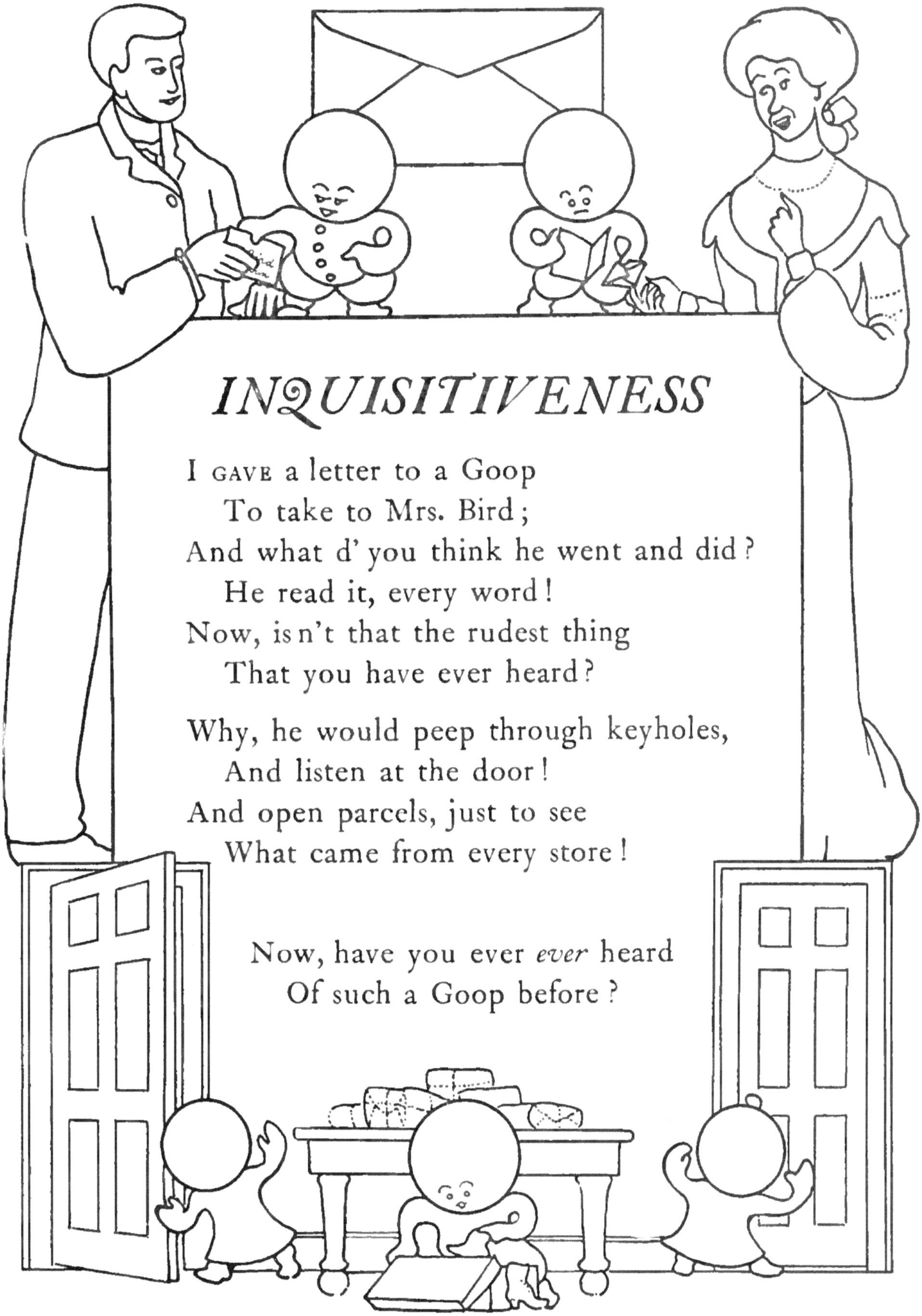

INQUISITIVENESS

I GAVE a letter to a Goop
To take to Mrs. Bird;
And what d' you think he went and did?
He read it, every word!
Now, isn't that the rudest thing
That you have ever heard?

Why, he would peep through keyholes,
And listen at the door!
And open parcels, just to see
What came from every store!

Now, have you ever *ever* heard
Of such a Goop before?

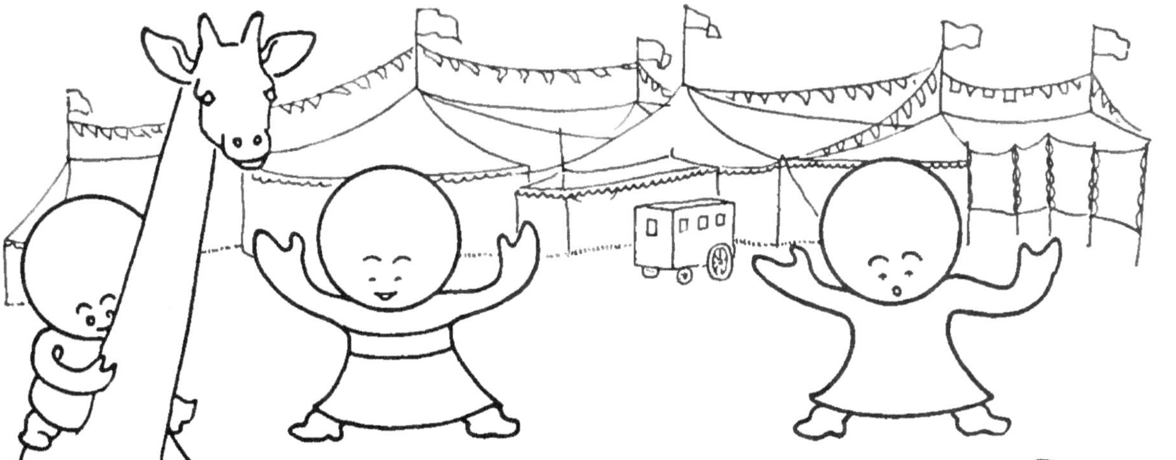

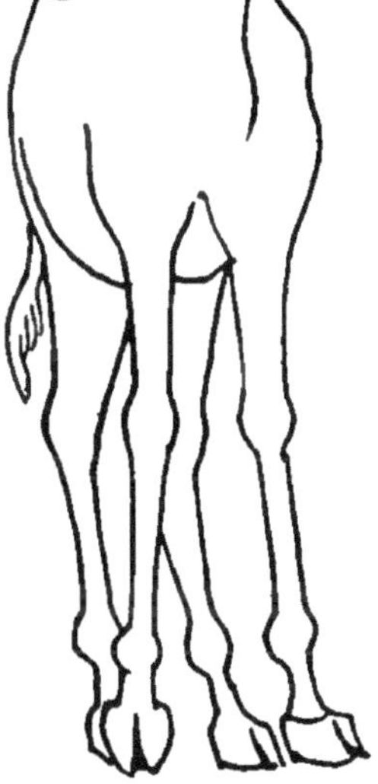

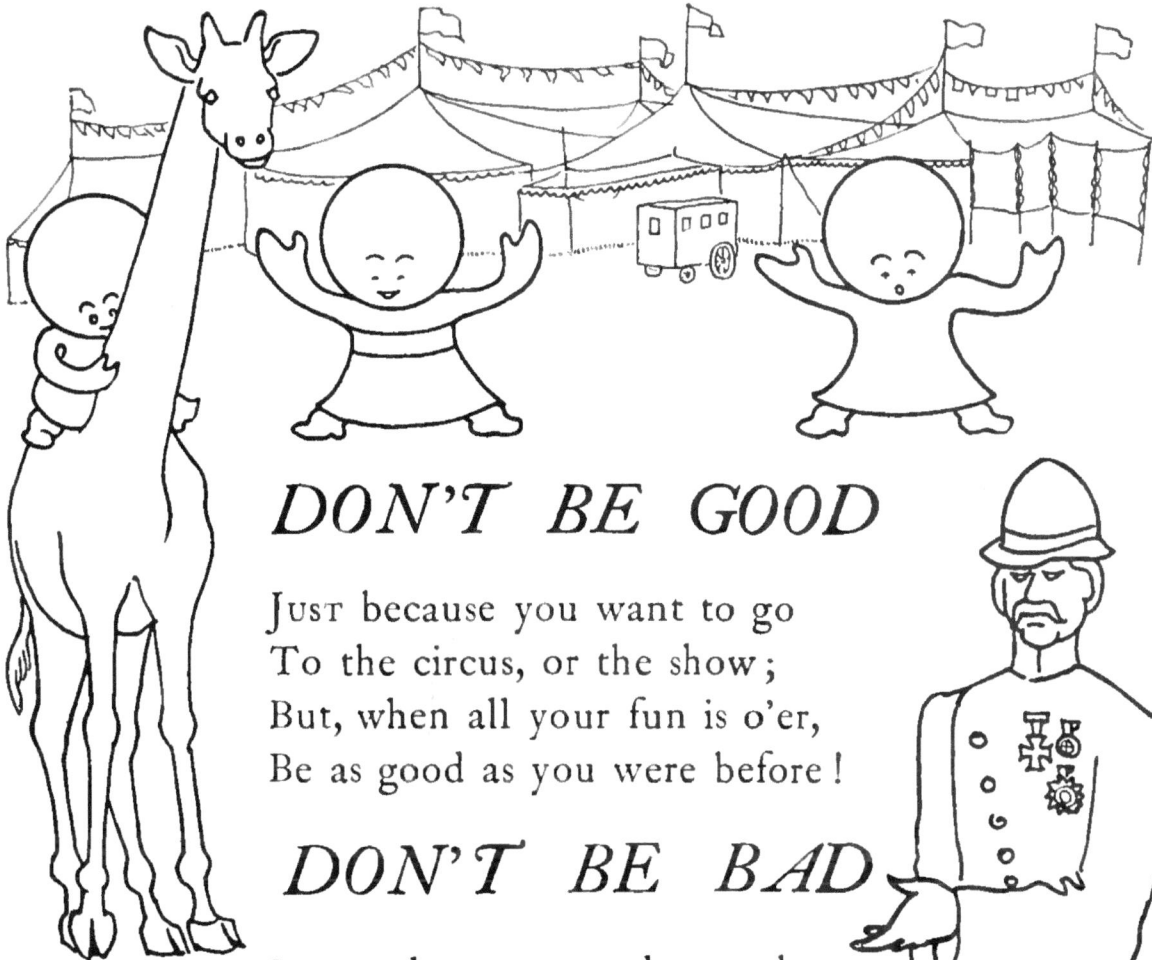

DON'T BE GOOD

Just because you want to go
To the circus, or the show;
But, when all your fun is o'er,
Be as good as you were before!

DON'T BE BAD

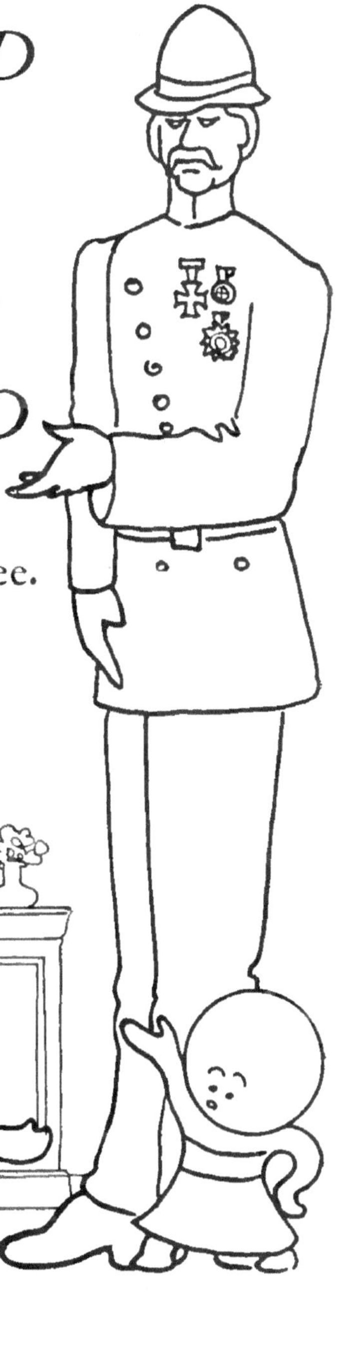

Just as long as you dare to be,
Because your mother does n't see.
Do not wait for her to scold,
But be just as good as gold!

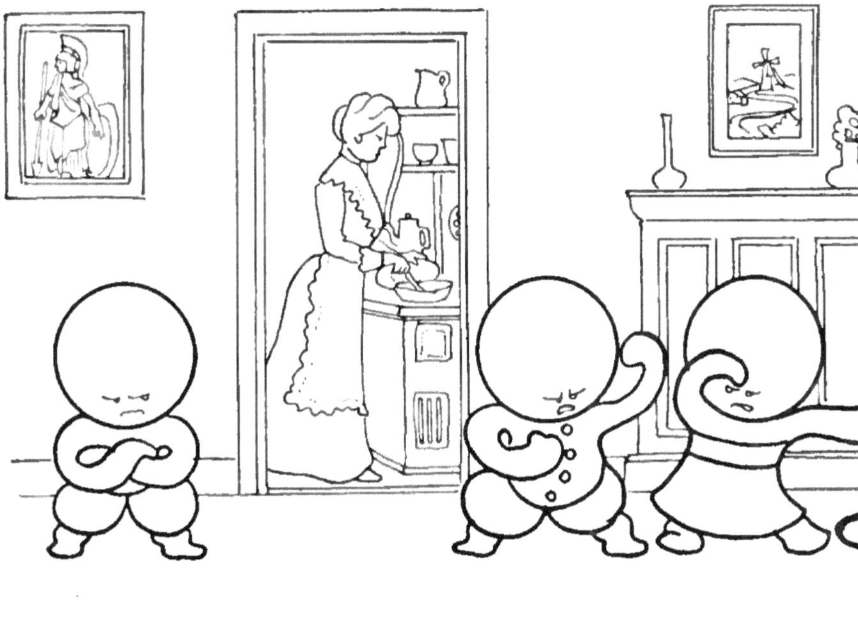

WRITE RIGHT!

If you were writing with your nose,
You'd *have* to curl up, I suppose,
And lay your head upon your hand;
But now, I cannot understand,
For you are writing with your pen!
So sit erect, and smile again!
You need not scowl because you write,
Nor hold your fingers *quite* so tight!
And if you gnaw the holder so,
      They'll take you for
      a Goop, you know!

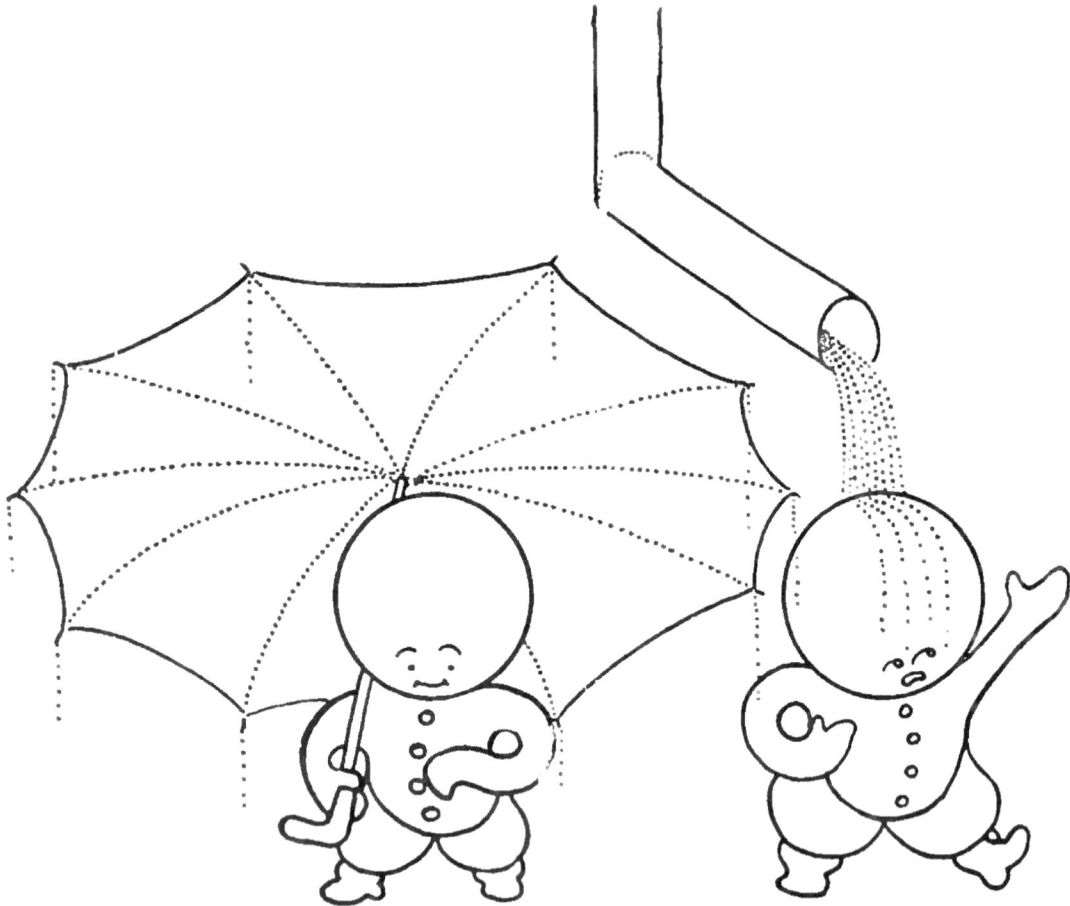

WET FEET

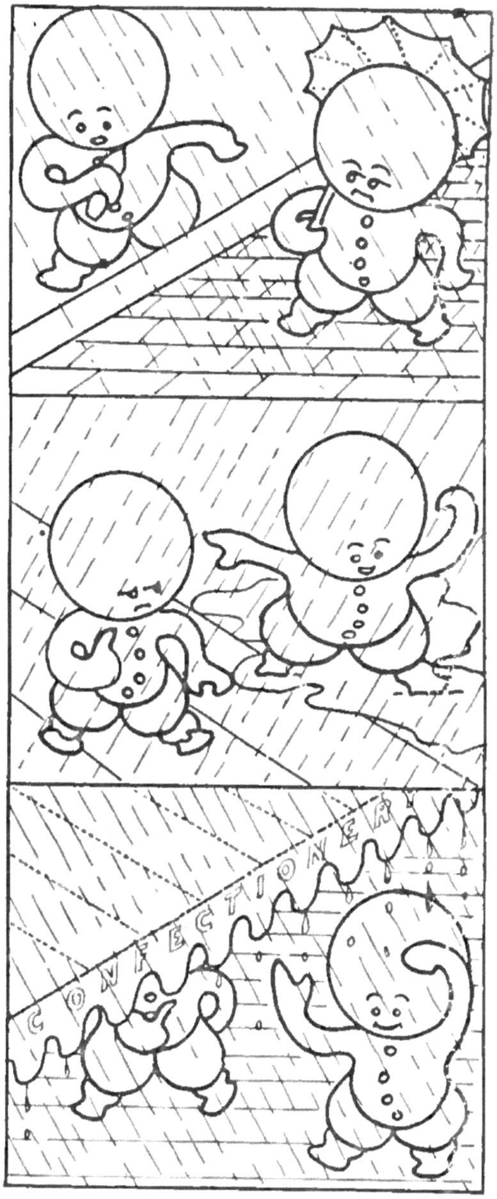
CONFECTIONER

Down the street together,
In the rainy weather,
Went a pair of little boys along;
One of them went straying
In the gutters playing,
Doing all his mother said was wrong;

One of them went dashing
Into puddles splashing,
Under dripping eaves that soaked him through;
One of them avoided
All the other boy did,
Dodging all the slimy, slushy goo.

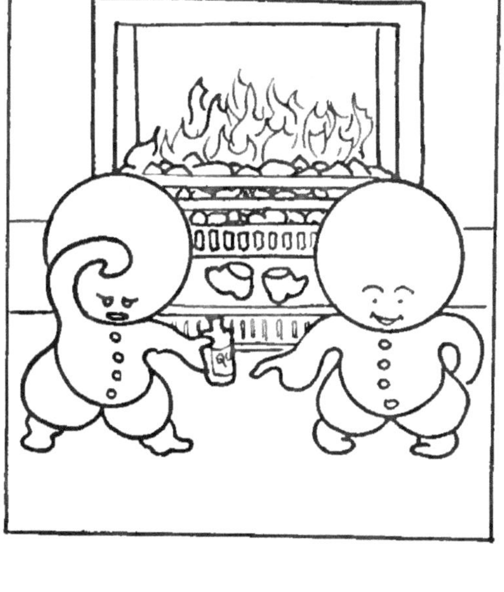

One of them grew chilly;
Said he felt so ill he
Knew he'd caught a cold, and coughed a lot!
The other was so warm he
Said he *liked* it stormy!
Which of them was Goop, and which was not?

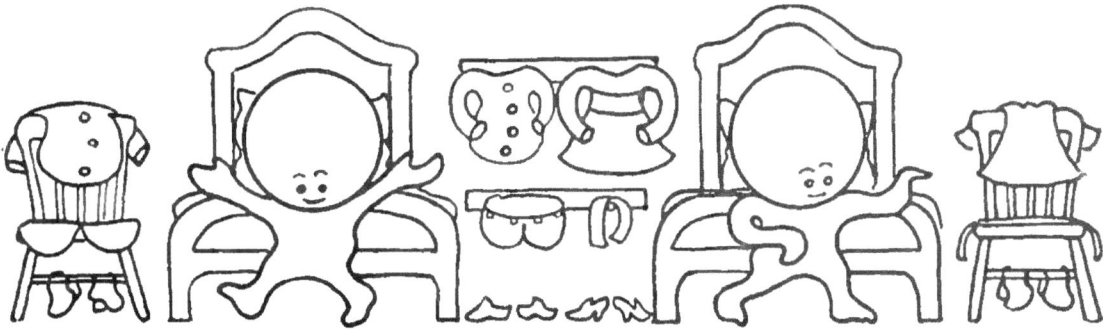

DRESS QUICKLY!

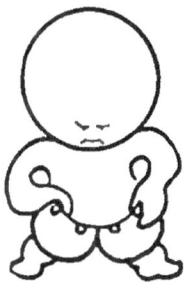

ALL your life you'll have to dress,
Every single day (unless
You should happen to be sick),
Why not learn to do it quick?
Hang your clothes the proper way,
So you'll find them fresh next day;
Treat them with a little care,
Fold them neatly on a chair;
So, without a bit of worry,
You can dress in quite a hurry.
Think of the slovenly Goops, before
You strew your clothing on the floor!

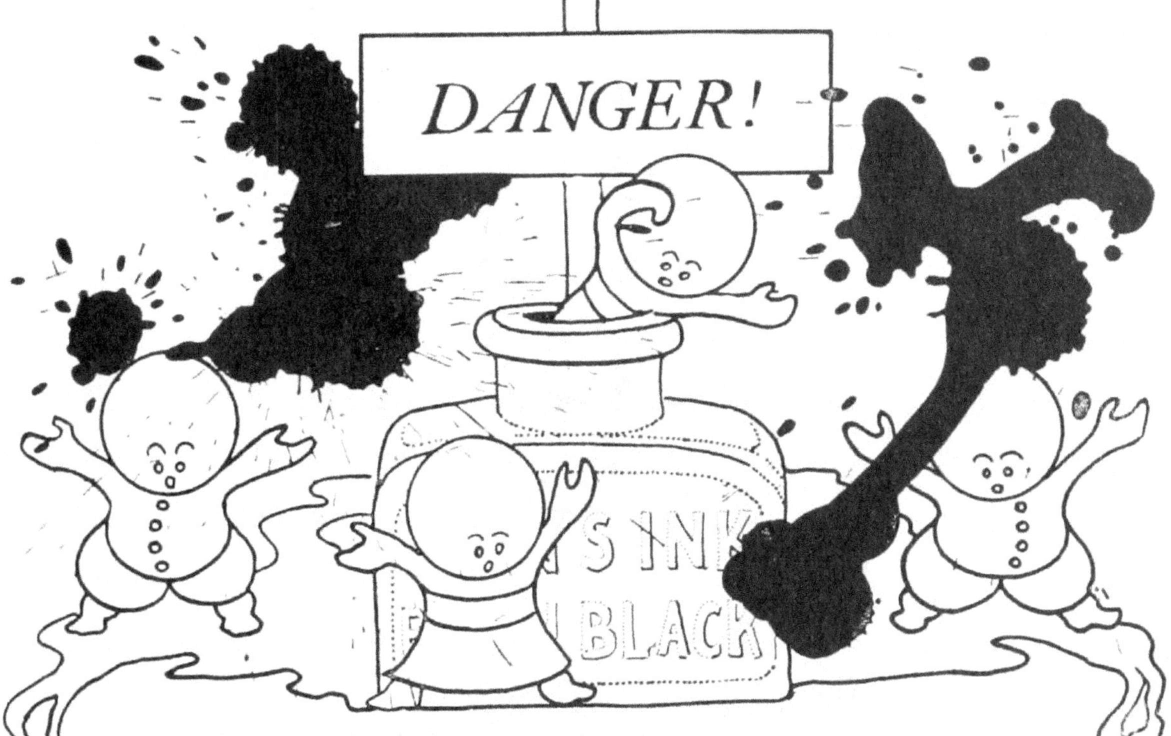
DANGER!
S INK
BLACK

INK, ink! What do you think!
You're sure to be stained, if you play with the ink!
You're sure to get black, if you play with the ink-well,
Before you begin it, just stop once, and think well!
All over your fingers, all over your face,
All over your clothes, and all over the place!
Your mother'll be angry, your father'll say, "*There!*
I said not to touch it; you said you'd take care!"

When Goops are so mischievous, they have to drink
Forty-four dozen bottles of raven black ink!

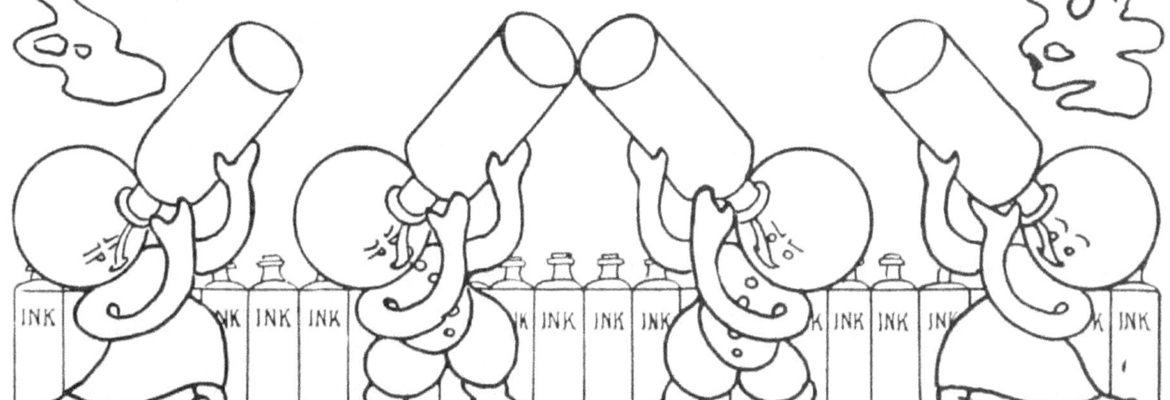
INK

THE REASON WHY

EVERYBODY liked Ezekiel.
  Why?
You could scarcely find his equal.
  Why?
If he made a mistake,
  He said he was wrong;
If he went on an errand,
  He wasn't gone long;
He never would bully,
  Although he was strong!

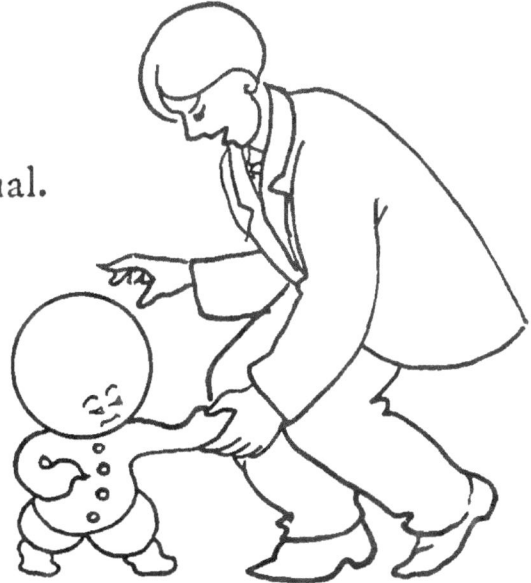

Everybody hated Mello.
  Why?
He was such a surly fellow.
  Why?
If you asked him for candy,
  He'd hide his away;
He never would play
  What the rest wished to play;
He would say *horrid* words
  That he ought n't to say!

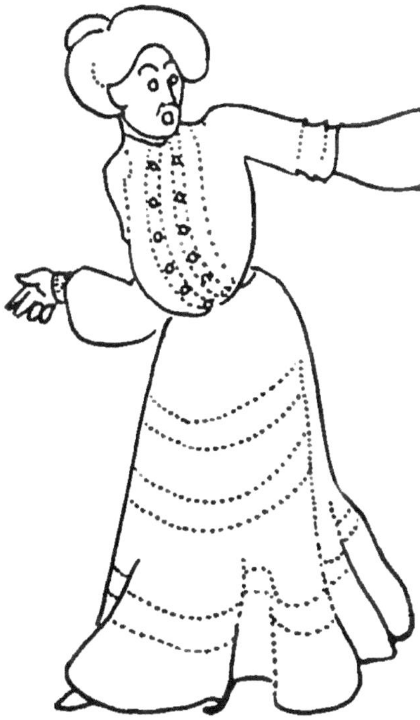

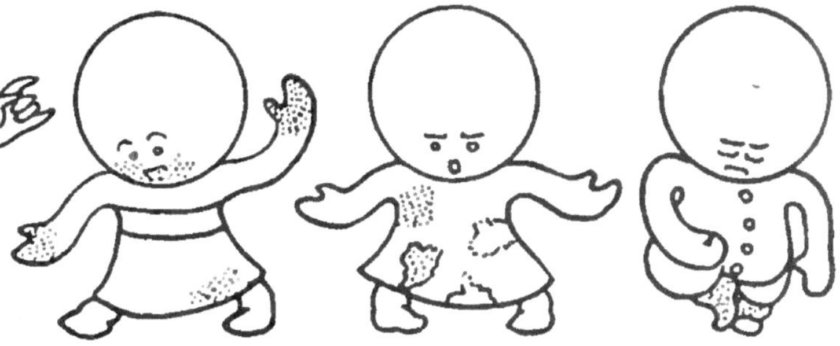

IN GOOP ATTIRE

I'll make you a dress of a towel,
  And trim it all over with soap,
With a sponge for a hat
And a wet one, at that!
  And *then* you 'll be happy, I hope!
You may act like a Goop, if you please,
In garments constructed like these!

But now, while you 're dressed up so neatly,
  Don't wipe off your hands on your frock!
The smooching that lingers
When you wipe off your fingers,
  Will give your dear mother a shock!
The result
will be
even more
shocking,
If you wipe off your
shoes on your
stocking!

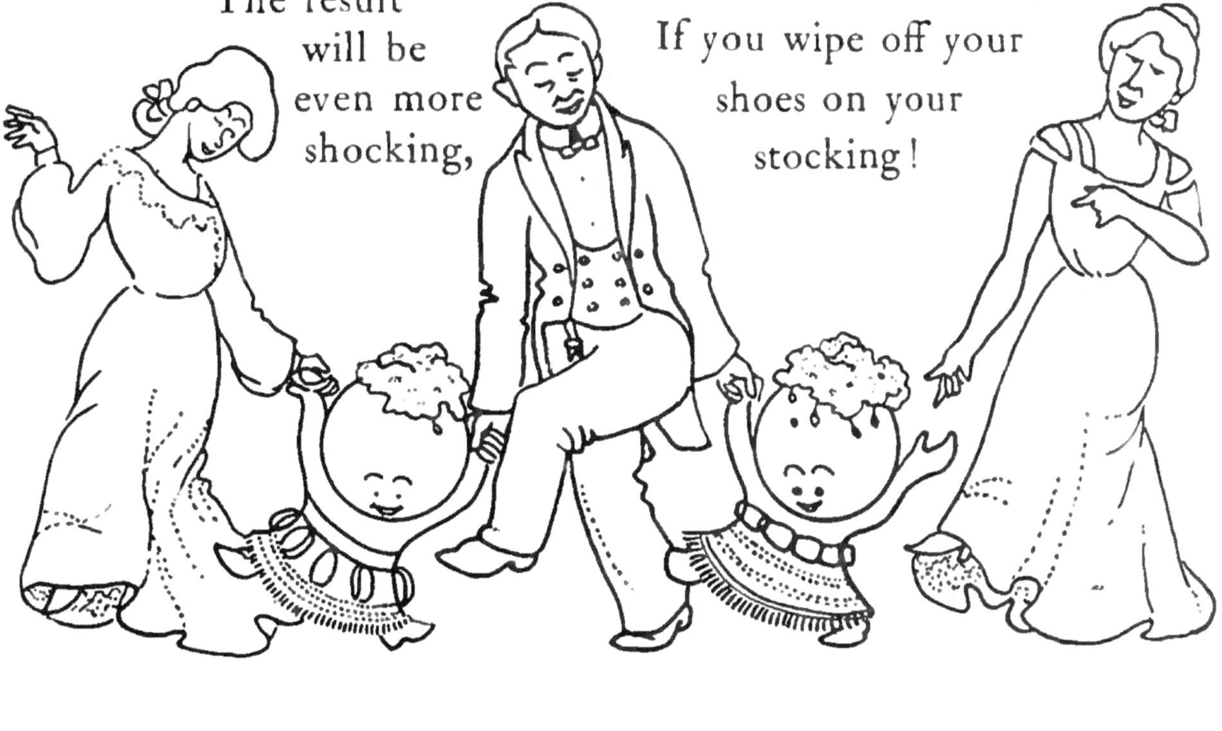

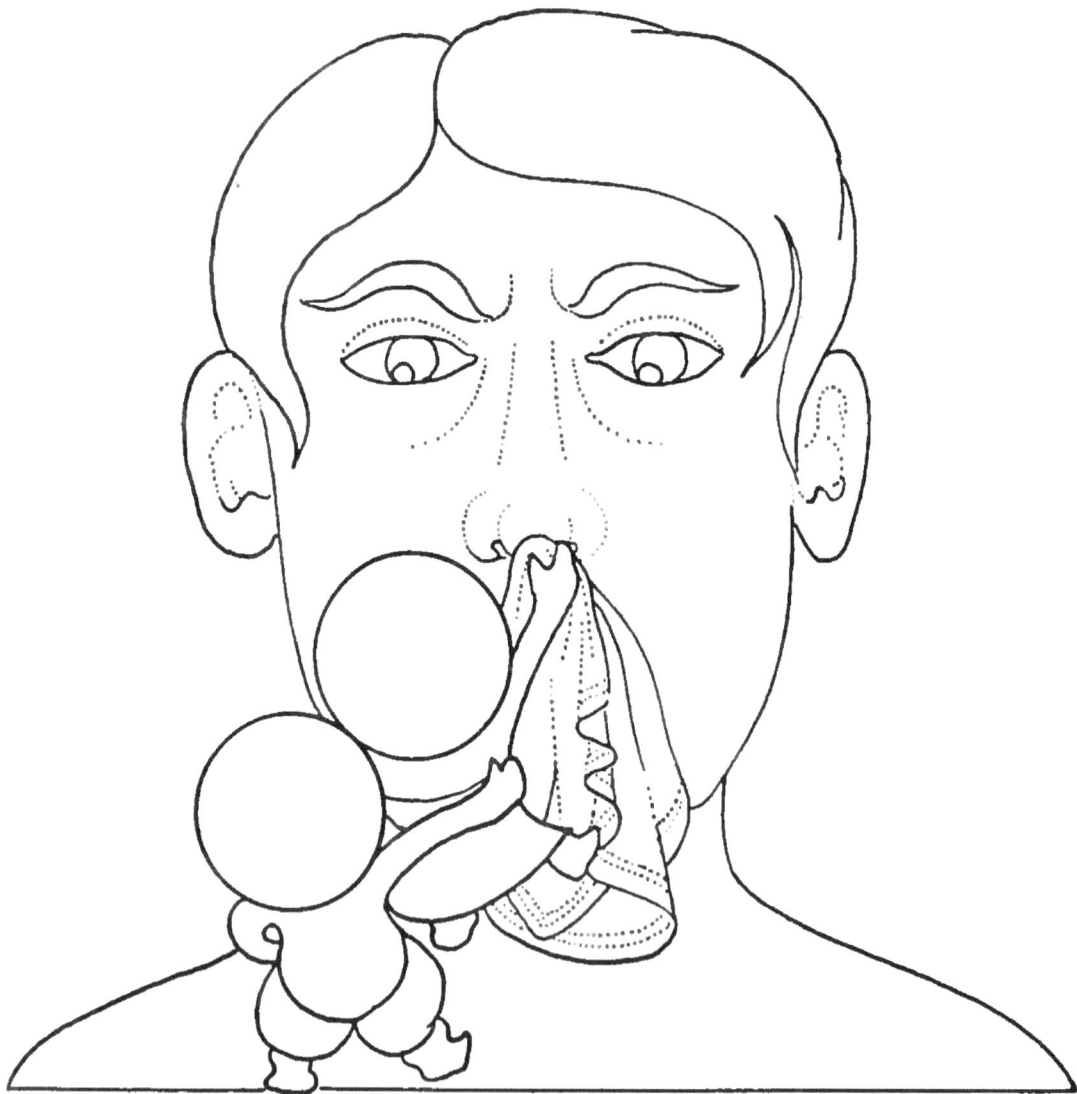

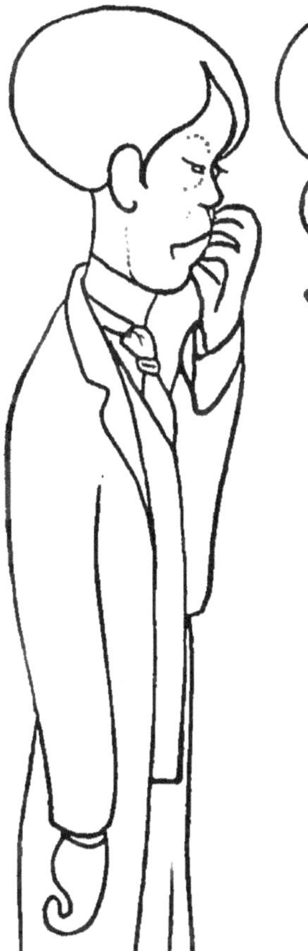

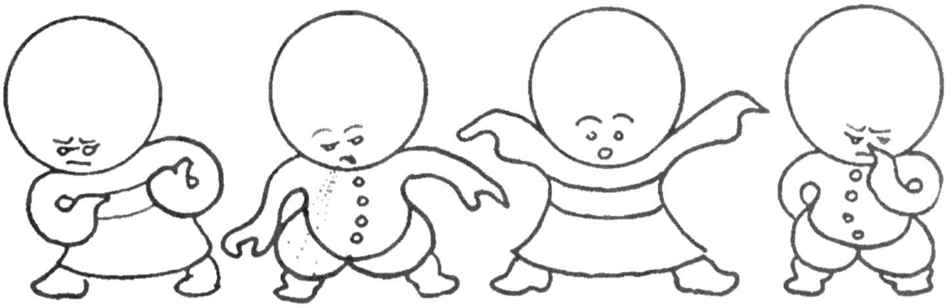

IMPOSSIBLE!

There once was a Goop (*it is hard to believe*
Such unpleasant behavior of you!)
Who always was wiping his nose on his sleeve;
I hope that this Goop was n't you!
He always was spitting (for fun, I suppose),
I could n't believe it of you!
And putting his fingers up into his nose;
I KNOW that this Goop was n't you!

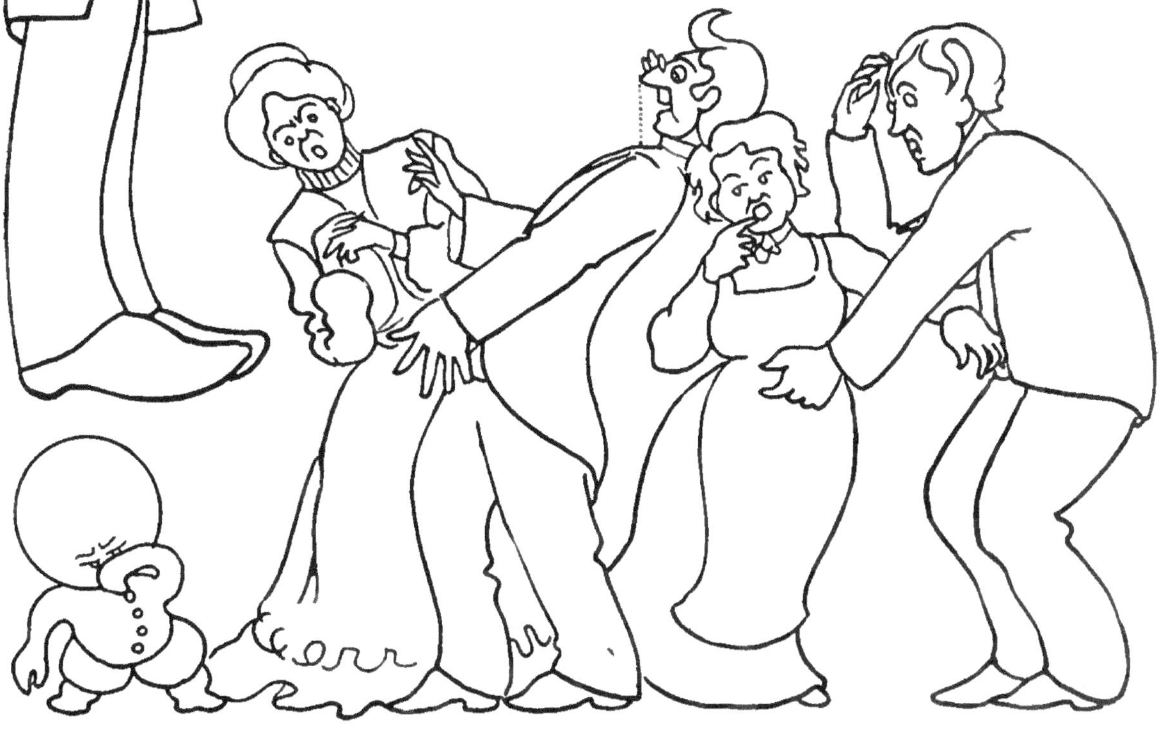

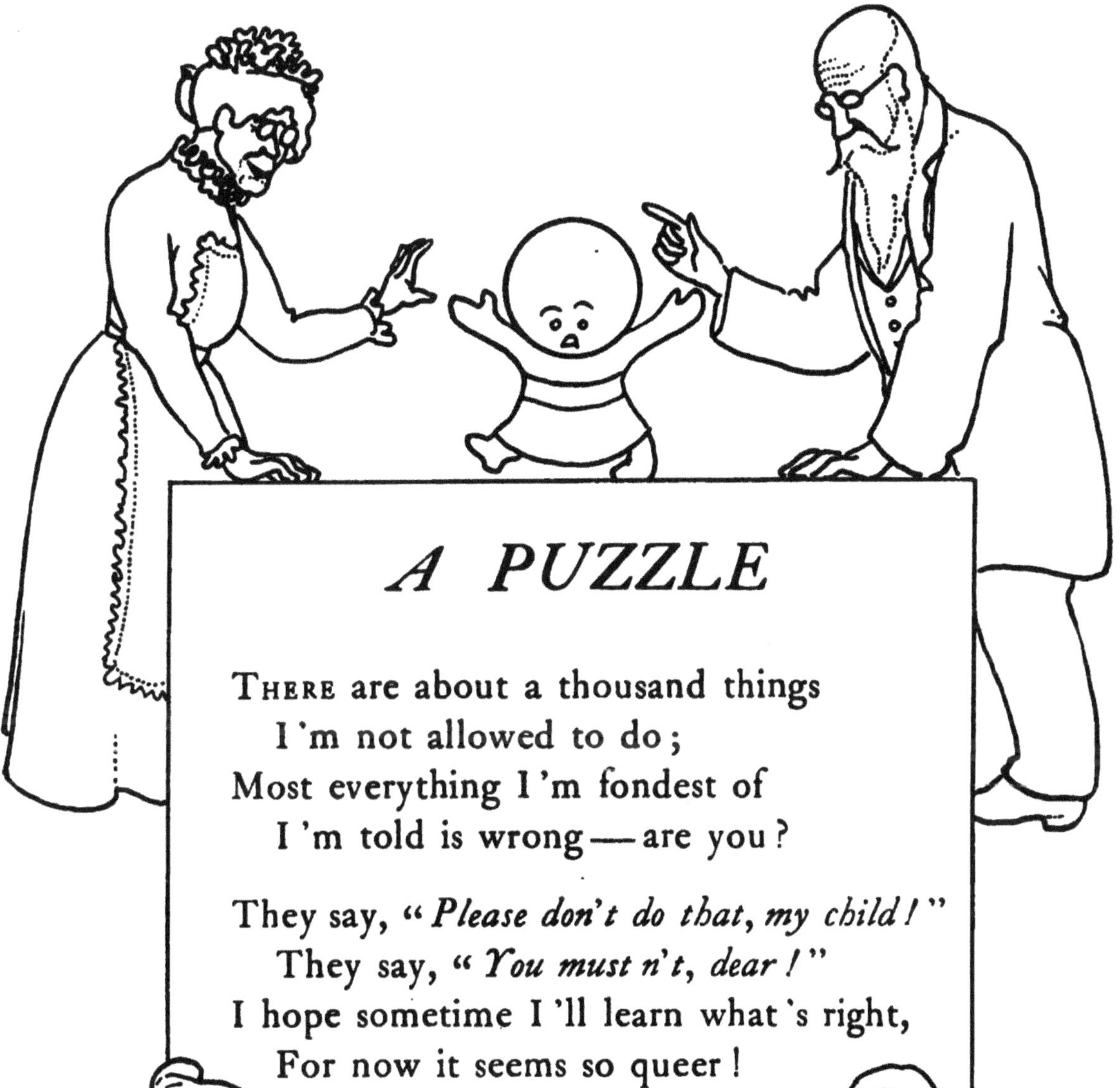

A PUZZLE

THERE are about a thousand things
  I 'm not allowed to do;
Most everything I 'm fondest of
  I 'm told is wrong — are you?

They say, "*Please don't do that, my child!*"
  They say, "*You must n't, dear!*"
I hope sometime I 'll learn what 's right,
  For now it seems so queer!

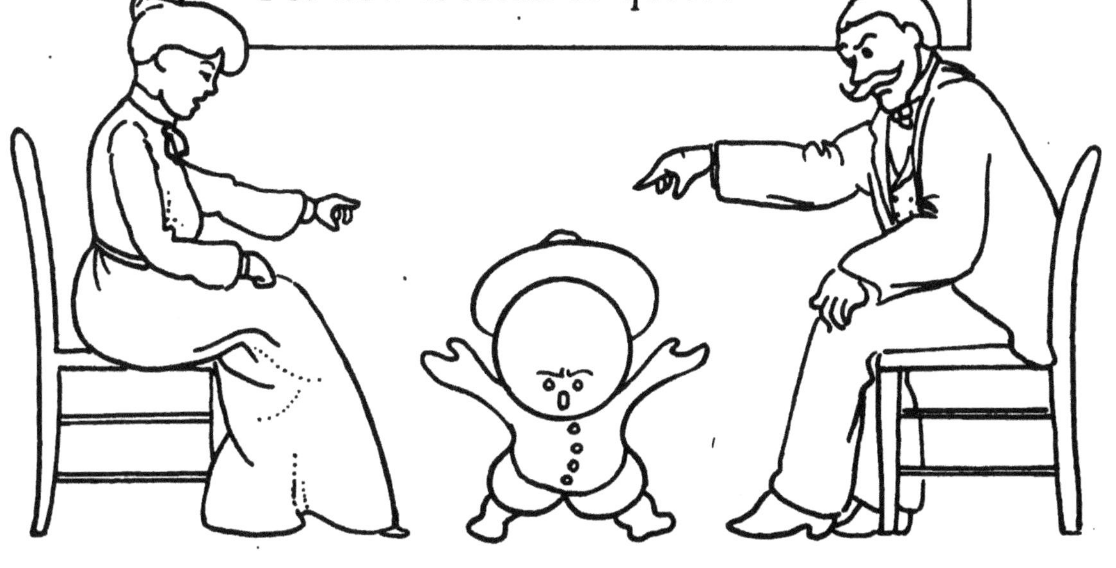

1903

AN

LPHABET

OF

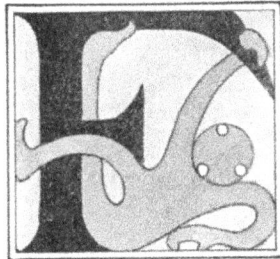AMOUS

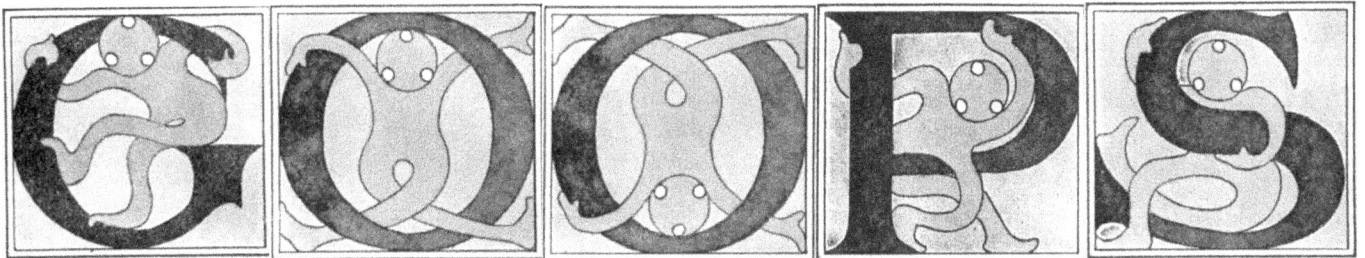

Taken from *The Burgess Nonsense Book*
Published by Frederick A. Stokes Company in 1901.

AN ALPHABET OF FAMOUS GOOPS.
Which you'll Regard with Yells and Whoops.
Futile Acumen!
For you Yourselves are Doubtless Dupes
Of Failings Such as Mar these Groups —
We all are Human!

ABEDNEGO was Meek and Mild; he Softly Spoke, he Sweetly Smiled.
He never Called his Playmates Names, and he was Good in Running Games;
But he was Often in Disgrace because he had a Dirty Face!

BOHUNKUS would Take Off his Hat, and Bow and Smile, and
Things like That.

His Face and Hair were Always Neat, and when he Played he
did not Cheat;

*But Oh! what Awful Words he Said, when it was Time to Go
to Bed!*

The Gentle CEPHAS tried his Best to Please his Friends with
Merry Jest;

He tried to Help Them, when he Could, for CEPHAS, he was
Very Good;

*And Yet — They Say he Used to Cry, and Once or Twice he Told
a Lie!*

DANIEL and DAGO were a Pair who Acted Kindly Every-
where;
They studied Hard, as Good as Gold, they Always did as
They were Told;
They Never Put on Silly Airs, *but They Took Things that were
Not Theirs.*

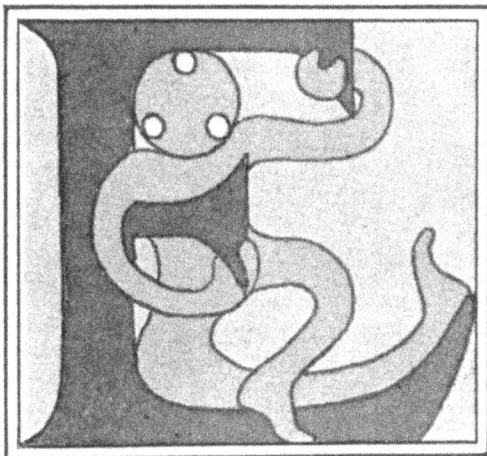

EZEKIEL, so his Parents said, just Simply *Loved* to Go to
Bed;
He was as Quiet as could Be whenever there were Folks to
Tea;
*And yet, he had a Little Way of Grumbling, when he should
Obey.*

When FESTUS was but Four Years Old his Parents Seldom
    had to Scold;
They never Called him " FESTUS DON'T ! " he Never Whined
    and said " *I Won't !* "
Yet it was Sad to See him Dine.   His Table Manners were Not
    Fine.

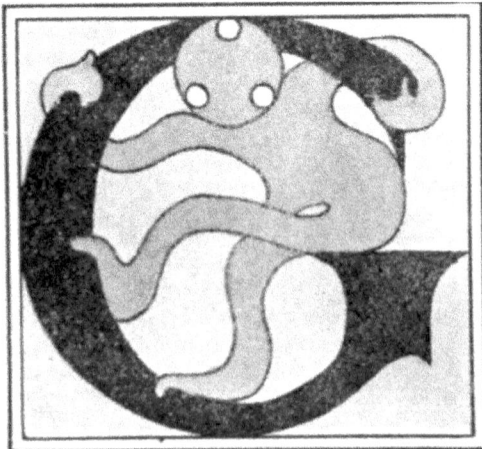

GAMALIEL took Peculiar Pride in Making Others Satisfied.
One Time I asked him for his Head. " *Why, Certainly !* "
    GAMALIEL Said.
He was Too Generous, in Fact. *But Bravery he Wholly*
    Lacked.

HAZAEL was (at Least he *Said* he Was) Exceedingly Well
   Bred ;
Forbidden Sweets he would not Touch, though he might Want
   them very Much.
But Oh, Imagination Fails to quite Describe his Finger Nails!

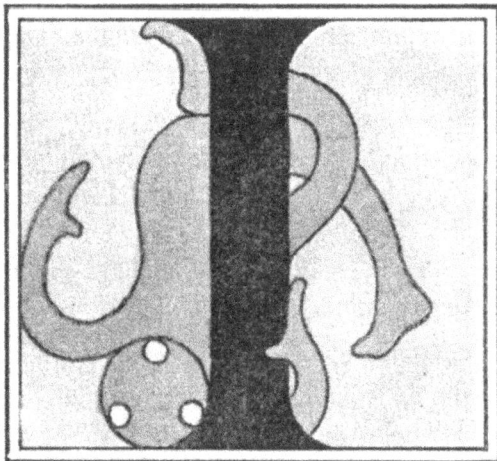

How Interesting ISAAC Seemed !   He never Fibbed, he Sel-
   dom Screamed ;
His Company was Quite a Treat to all the Children on the
   Street ;
*But Nurse has Told me of his Wrath when he was Made to Take
   a Bath !*

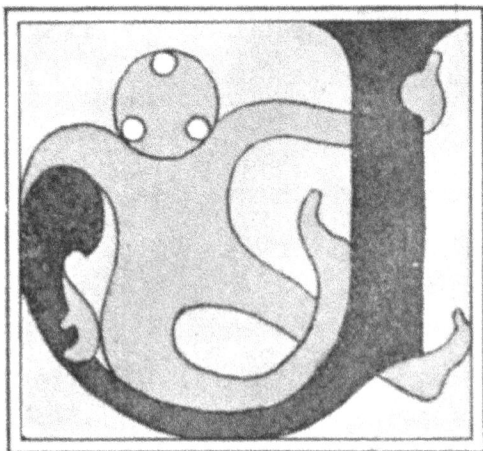

Oh, Think of JONAH when you're Bad; Think what a Happy Way he had

Of Saying " *Thank You!* " — " *If you Please* " — " *Excuse Me, Sir,* " and Words like These.

Still, he was Human, like Us All. His Muddy Footprints Tracked the Hall.

Just fancy KADESH for a Name! Yet he was Clever All the Same;

He knew Arithmetic, at Four, as Well as Boys of Nine or More!

But I Prefer far Duller Boys, who do Not Make such Awful Noise!

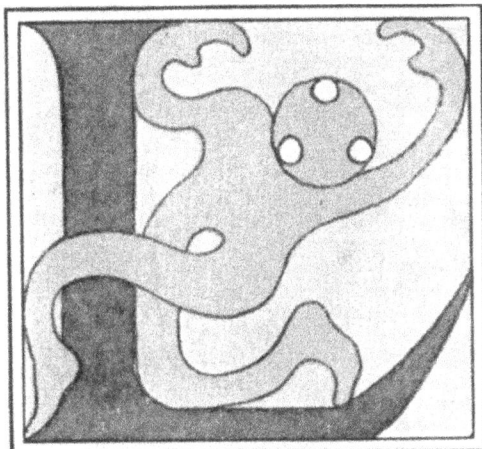

Oh, Laugh at LABAN, if you Will, but he was Brave when he
was Ill.

When he was Ill, he was so Brave he Swallowed All his
Mother Gave!

*But Somehow, She could never Tell why he was Worse when he
was Well!*

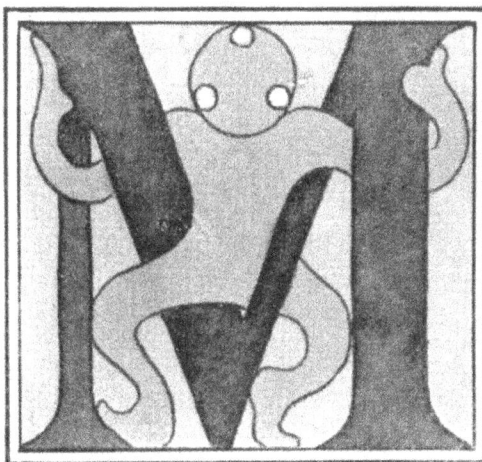

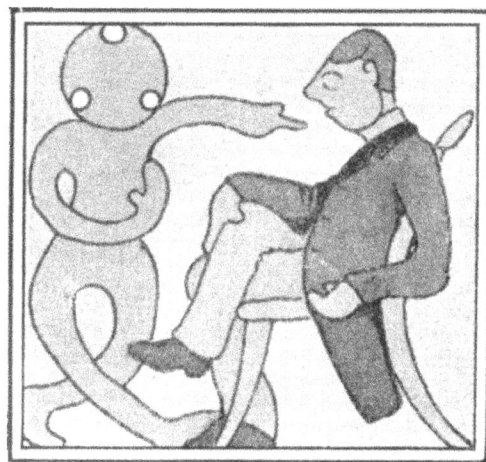

If MICAH's Mother Told him "*No*" he Made but Little of
his Woe;

He Always Answered, "*Yes, I'll Try!*" for MICAH Thought
it Wrong to Cry.

*Yet he was Always Asking Questions and Making quite Ill-timed
Suggestions.*

I Fancy NICODEMUS Knew as Much as I, or even You;

He was Too Careful, I am Sure, to Scratch or Soil the Furniture;

He never Squirmed, he never Squalled; *he Never Came when he was Called!*

Some think that OBADIAH's Charm was that he Never Tried to Harm

Dumb Animals in any Way, though Some are Cruel when they Play.

But though he was so Sweet and Kind, his Mother found him Slow to Mind.

When PELEG had a Penny Earned, to Share it with his Friends
   he Yearned.
And if he Bought a Juicy Fig, his Sister's Half was Very Big!
Had he not Hated to Forgive, he would have been Too Good to
   Live!

When QUARTO's brother QUARTO Hit, was QUARTO Angry?
   Not a Bit!
He Called the Blow a Little Joke, and so Affectionately Spoke,
That Everybody Loved the Lad.   *Yet Oh, What Selfish Ways*
   he Had!

Was REUBEN Happy? I should Say! He laughed and Sang the Livelong Day.

He Made his Mother Smile with Joy to See her Sunny-Tempered Boy.

However, she was Not so Gay when REUB *Refused to Stop his Play!*

When SHADRACH Cared to be Polite, they Called him Gentlemanly, Quite;

His Manners were Correct and Nice; he Never Asked for Jelly Twice!

Still, when he Tried to Misbehave, O, how Much Trouble SHADRACH *Gave!*

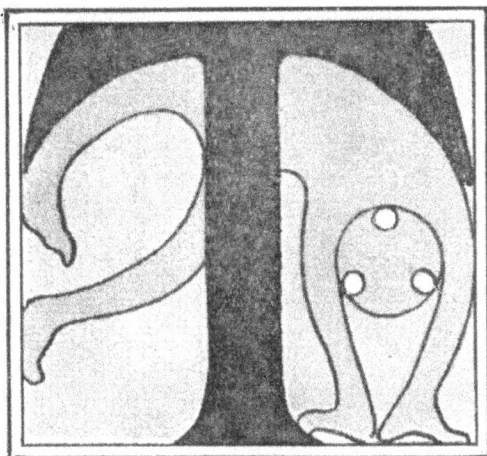

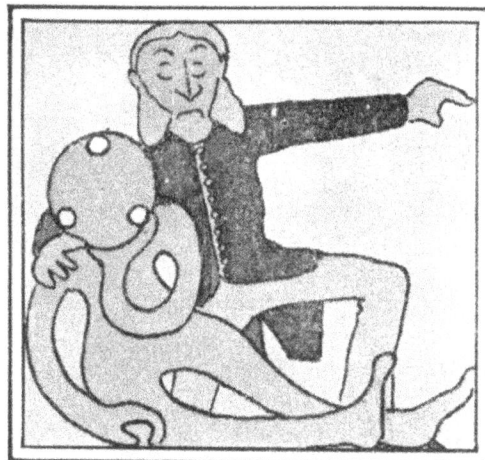

Don't Think that TIMOTHY was Ill because he Sometimes Kept so Still.

He knew his Mother Did Not Care to Hear him Talking Everywhere.

He did not Tease, he did Not Cry, *but he was Always Asking* "WHY?"

URIAH Never Licked his Knife, nor Sucked his Fingers, in his Life.

He Never Reached, to Help Himself, the Sugar Bowl upon the Shelf.

He Never Popped his Cherry Pits; *but he had Horrid Sulky Fits!*

To See young VIVIUS at his Work, you Knew he'd Never Try to Shirk.

The Most Unpleasant Things he'd Do, if but his Mother Asked him To.

But when young Vivius Grew Big, it Seems he was a Norful Prig!

Why WABAN always Seemed so Sweet, was that he Kept so Clean and Neat.

He never Smooched his Face with Coal, his Picture Books were Fresh and Whole.

He washed His Hands Ten Times a Day; *but, Oh, what Horrid Words he'd Say!*

What shall I say of XENOGOR, Save that he Always Shut the Door!

He always Put his Toys Away when he had Finished with his Play.

But here his List of Virtues Ends.   A Tattle-Tale does not Make Friends.

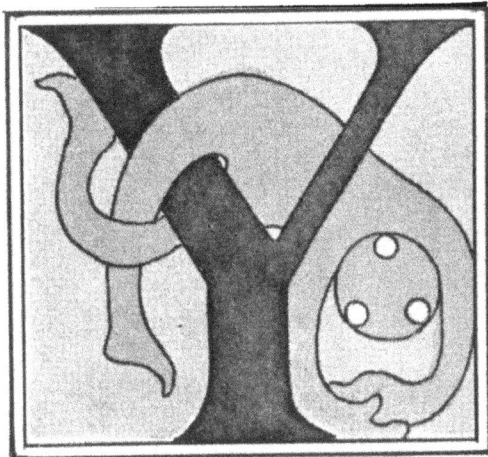

YERO was Noted for the Way with which he Helped his Comrades Play;

He'd Lend his Cart, he'd Lend his Ball, his Marbles, and his Tops and All!

And Yet (I Doubt if you'll Believe), he Wiped his Nose upon his Sleeve!

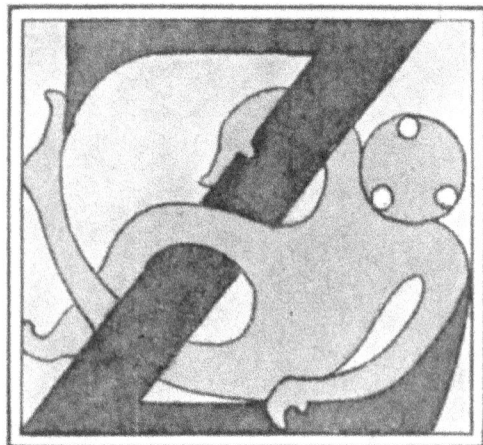

The Zealous ZIBEON was Such as Casual Callers Flatter Much.

His Maiden Aunts would Say, with Glee, " How Good, how Pure, how Dear is He ! "

And Yet, he Drove his Mother Crazy — he was so Slow, he was so Lazy !

FINIS

SO ENDS THE TOME: ARE YOU, MY FRIEND,
AS GLAD AS I TO SEE THE END?
HAVE YOU DONNED MOTLEY FOR THE MONEY
AND FEARED YOUR JESTS WERE NONE TOO FUNNY?
SO ENDS THE TOME: SO ENDS MY FOLLY;
'TIS DISMAL WORK, THIS BEING JOLLY.
NO MORE I'LL PLAY THE HARLEQUIN
UNLESS MORE ROYALTIES COME IN.

St. Augustine Academy Press

...because what children read really matters...

At St. Augustine Academy Press, we are committed to publishing only the best children's literature of yesterday and today.

If you enjoyed our Collection of Goops, here are some other books you might like:

Laugh yourself silly as you learn how <u>not</u> to behave in Church!

Do your parents cringe while you pound your feet on the pews? Do you pester them all through Church with questions and demands? Do the folks in the pews around you stare? Then this book is for you! Never was there a more fun way to learn the do's and don'ts of Church behavior than this hilarious collection of antics that demonstrates how NOT to act!

Inspired by Gellett Burgess' Goops, author Lisa Bergman insists that her children never, never behave like these hooligans...(well, *hardly* ever, that is)...Meanwhile, talented teen Erin Bartholomew brings out the best of these crazy kids with her illustrations, from Backwards Buford to Potty Prue. If you liked the Goops, you'll love this book!

A recent perusal of a modern set of encyclopedias revealed a mere three-line entry for Roland, whose story formed the basis for one of the first great epics of medieval France, the *Chanson de Roland.* So much of western culture was born from this legend, and yet most young people today have never even heard of him.

Books like *Page, Esquire and Knight* are the perfect antidote to this lack. Condensed from such classics as Malory's *Morte d'Arthur,* the Arthurian poems of Tennyson, and the original *Chanson de Roland,* it gives young people a solid introduction to these giants of literature which is sure to inspire a lasting interest. Included are tales of King Arthur's knights, the battles of Charlemagne, Godfrey de Bouillon and The Crusades, St. George and the Dragon, and Pierre Terrail LeVieux, the famed Chevalier du Bayard. Engagingly written and enhanced by vivid illustrations, *Page, Esquire and Knight* is sure to be attractive to both boys and girls, young and old.

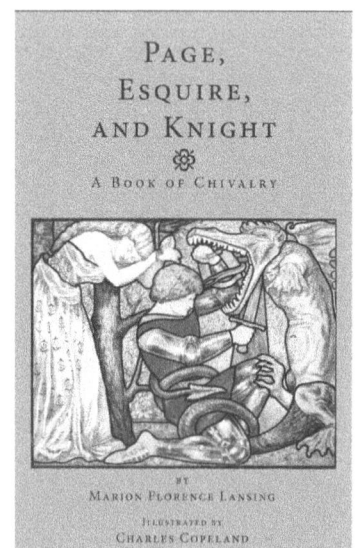

Discover these books and more at www.staugustineacademypress.com

www.ingramcontent.com/pod-product-compliance
Lightning Source LLC
Chambersburg PA
CBHW080700110426

42739CB00034B/3347